Resisting the Devil with a Steadfast Faith

by George Gifford

with chapters by C. Matthew McMahon

Copyright Information

Resisting the Devil with a Steadfast Faith, by George Gifford, with chapters by C. Matthew McMahon
Edited by Susan Ruth and Therese B. McMahon

Copyright ©2020 by Puritan Publications and A Puritan's Mind

Some language and grammar have been updated from the original manuscript. Any change in wording or punctuation has not changed the intent or meaning of the original author(s), and has been made to aid the modern reader.

Published by Puritan Publications
A Ministry of A Puritan's Mind ®
Crossville, TN
www.puritanpublications.com
www.apuritansmind.com

All rights reserved. No part of this publication may be reproduced, stored in a retrieval system or transmitted in any form by any means, electronic, mechanical, photocopy, recording or otherwise, without the prior permission of the publisher, except as provided by USA copyright law.

Manufactured in the United States of America

eISBN: 978-1-62663-376-6
ISBN: 978-1-62663-377-3

Table of Contents

The Devil and Evil Angels 4

Meet George Gifford 13

Preface 22

Resist Steadfast in the Faith 25

Can One Lose a Steadfast Faith? 62

Other Helpful Works Published by Puritan Publications 92

The Devil and Evil Angels
by C. Matthew McMahon, Ph.D. Th.D.

"Submit yourselves therefore to God. Resist the devil, and he will flee from you," (James 4:7).

Satan in Scripture is called Abaddon, (Rev. 9:11); the accuser of the brethren, (Rev. 12:10); adversary, (1 Peter 5:8); angel of the bottomless pit, (Rev. 9:11); Apollyon, (Rev. 9:11); Beelzebub, (Matt. 12:24; Mark 3:22; Luke 11:15); Belial, (2 Cor. 6:15); the devil, (Matt. 4:1; Luke 4:2, 6; Rev. 20:2); enemy, (Matt. 13:39); an evil spirit, (1 Sam. 16:14); the father of lies, (John 8:44); the great red dragon, (Rev. 12:3); *the* liar, (John 8:44); a lying spirit, (1 Kings 22:22); a murderer, (John 8:44); that old serpent, (Rev. 12:9; 20:2); the power of darkness, (Col. 1:13); the prince of this world, (John 12:31; 14:30; 16:11); the prince of devils, (Matt. 12:24); the prince of the power of the air, (Eph. 2:2); the ruler of the darkness of this world, (Eph. 6:12); Satan, (1 Chr. 21:1; Job 1:6; John 13:27; Acts 5:3; 26:18; Rom. 16:20); the serpent, (Gen. 3:4, 14; 2 Cor. 11:3); the spirit that works in the children of disobedience, (Eph. 2:2); tempter, (Matt. 4:3; 1 Thess. 3:5); the god of this world, (2 Cor. 4:4); unclean spirit, (Matt. 12:43); and the wicked one, (Matt. 13:19, 38). As you can see, Scripture does *not* deny his existence, but rather, substantiates it as the great opposer to the people of God, the great liar and tempter who combats God's will and word. When the devil speaks, he slanders, which is his main language (Rev. 12:10). He is devoid of truth, and desires the complete and utter destruction of the church, and the abasement of the glory of God (John 8:44).

The devil is the church's adversary, burning with hatred for both God and man (Rev. 12:9). He is the adversary of the Christ, and the adversary to all the good creatures which the Lord had made. He is the adversary dead set against God, all good men, and all good actions which stem from the perceptive will of God found in Scripture. If he had free license from God to act, (though he is wholly subjugated to God (Job 1-2)) he would seek to destroy them all, (as he did the heard of swine) that neither the Lord should have the glory of that manifold goodness, which appears in his creatures, and neither should man have their comfort and benefit.

The devil is, in his own nature, corrupt, and most evil, being the head and captain of all evil people (of both devils and men) and the instigator and furtherer of evil purposes and works, (John 17:15; Matt. 5:37, 6:13, 19; 1 John 2:13). He desires to resist God's will at every turn, and to cause others to do so as well (Gen. 3:1ff, 24:50, 31:24), leading them off and away from the road of salvation.

The devil is evil, not in substance or person, but in nature or quality. He is not evil by *creation* from God, but by voluntary departure from God and goodness. He is perfectly evil, but not infinitely evil. He is evil into all eternity, but not evil from all eternity. This may be said of all those whose father is the devil, that they too are evil, but not perfectly evil, nor from eternity, nor to eternity. The devil, and his angels, do not possess the infinite nature of God, and cannot be, nor are, infinitely evil; they are *utterly* evil in all the do. Where did these fallen angels come from?

The Bible teaches that certain angels did not keep their first estate in heaven and sinned (Jude 1:6). These are denominated unclean spirits, principalities, powers, rulers of this world, and spiritual wickednesses (*i.e.*, wicked spirits) in high places. The most common designation given to them collectively is *demons* or *devils*. Their original condition was holy. But they sinned and were cast out of heaven. When they fell, the particular nature of their sin is not specifically revealed, though it surrounded pride, as found in 1 Tim. 3:6, "...Not a novice, lest being lifted up with pride he fall into the condemnation of the devil." Paul directs Timothy that a pastor must not be "a novice, *lest being lifted up with pride* he fall into the condemnation of the devil." This is interpreted as the condemnation which the devil incurred for the same sin.

Fallen angels will ultimately be condemned and sent to hell. "...he hath reserved in everlasting chains under darkness unto the judgment of the great day," (Jude 1:6). There is, among these fallen angels, one fallen angel exalted in rank and power above all others called Satan (the adversary), the evil one. His titles set him forth as the great enemy of righteousness, the opposer of all that is good and the promoter of all that is evil. Paul explains, "Lest Satan should get an advantage of us: for we are not ignorant of his devices," (2 Cor. 2:11).

This one wicked spirit, who of his malicious accusing God to Eve, when he tempted her, (Gen. 3:3-4) has been scripturally designated *the* devil, and chief accuser or slanderer. He is designated as *the* "evil one" the head of all unclean spirits (Matthew 6:13 more accurately translated "the evil one"). He is mentioned in the singular number, as elsewhere often throughout Scripture, having his angels *joined* to him, as seduced by him, and inferior to him. This is opposite to all good angels and elect men and women who are subject to Christ as their Head (Matthew 25:41). And wicked spirits have various names given to them in holy Scripture to designate and signify their *nature* as spirits, or their *office*. As good angels are sent forth as righteous messengers from God, wicked angels are sent out by the devil in their malice against God and men (such as called Satan, spiritual wickednesses, devils, dragon, serpents, *etc.*). Or they are designated by the actions, and their great might (as principalities, dominions, powers, *etc.*). Or by their effects, (as *unclean* spirits, *deaf* and *dumb* spirits, *father* of lies, murderer, *etc.*). The use of all this in Scripture is to designate their desires and intentions towards people, especially as tempters against believers, using all their wiles to stir up the true Christian to hate Christ and his works. Scripture demonstrates these truths that believers would be watchful, given to sobriety and prayer, (1 Peter 5:8).

Though evil spirits are represented as being exceedingly numerous and operating in nature and in the minds of men, they have specific limitations. They are dependent on God, and can act only under his control and by his permission. Martin Luther called the devil "God's barking dog." Evil angels are bound to the laws of nature, and they cannot interfere with the freedom and responsibility of men.

The most expressive operation of evil angels and the devil in human history have been the power of evil spirits over the bodies and minds of men. Today, they are great influencers of men, those who whisper in their ears to suggest opposition to the word of God, and who steal away the word of God from out of the heart of those that it might do good. In times past, their extensive operation included *demonic possession.* Possessions in the Bible are found in two ways: 1) Those in which the soul alone was the subject of the diabolic influence, as in the case of the "damsel possessed with a spirit of divination," mentioned in Acts 16:16. 2) Those in which the bodies alone, or as was more frequently the case, both the body and mind were the subjects of this spiritual influence. Jesus confronted on in Luke 8:26, as he did on many occasions, "And when he went forth to land, there met him out of the city a certain man, which had devils a long time, and ware no clothes, neither abode in any house, but in the tombs." The term *possession* means the inhabitation of an evil spirit in such relation to the body and soul as to exert a controlling influence, producing violent agitations and great suffering, both mental and corporeal. Such was the case of the sons of Sceva who were beaten. "And the man in whom the evil spirit was leaped on them, and overcame them, and prevailed against them, so that they fled out of that house naked and wounded," (Acts 19:16). Christ often healed people inhabited by demonic influence and possession, "They also which saw it told them by what means he that was possessed of the devils was healed," (Luke 8:36).

In the beginning, in the Genesis narrative (chapter 3), Adam and Eve were present at the first temptation given by the serpent, who was in fact possessed of the devil. In Genesis 3:6 it is said the woman gave of the fruit of the tree to her husband who was "with her." Satan was the real tempter and he used the serpent merely as his organ or instrument. A serpent may be the most subtle of all the beasts of the field but he does not have the high intellectual faculties which the tempter here demonstrates calling into question the integrity of God and knowing "what God said" or "didn't say." The Scriptures teach that Satan seduced our first parents into sin. In fact, he is the great deceiver of the world, as Rev. 12:9 says, "The great dragon was cast out, that old serpent, called the Devil, and Satan, which deceiveth the whole world." The Apostle Paul says in 2 Cor. 11:3 "I fear lest...as the serpent beguiled Eve through his subtlety, so also your minds should be corrupted from the simplicity that is in Christ." Paul believed that by the serpent was meant Satan's wiles, which is plain from verse 14, where he speaks of Satan as *the great deceiver*. Paul also alludes to Genesis 3:15 in Romans 16:20 when he says, "The God of peace shall bruise Satan under your feet." And Jesus Christ said in John 8:44, "Ye are of your father the devil, and the lusts of your father ye will do. He was a murderer from the beginning, and abode not in the truth, because there is no truth in him. When he speaketh a lie, he speaketh of his own: for he is a liar, and the father of it."

When people act in accordance with the devil, they sin, and become of a "devilish quality," (John 6:70). When they are enticed, they are pulled away from God by honors, profits, pleasures, or whatever other things the devil uses to hinder their profiting by the Word, (Luke 8:12). These wicked spirits have such a heinous effect on the world, that the same condemnation that will befall them, will befall those who follow them. 1 Tim. 3:6 states that the devil is condemned, and wicked men will also be condemned if they do not repent. The proud fall into the condemnation of the devil, that is, by means of pride and high mindedness they too will be cast into hell fire, in the same manner as the devil will be. To be devilish in following the father of lies, is to be "full" denoting the aim to keep a man in an unregenerate state. In this, "All worldly wisdom is proper to devils, or which is inspired by devils or evil spirits. This worldly wisdom is called devilish, both because it follows the devil, and is suggested and inspired by him; doing all that which the devil practices, (Job 1:10-11; Rev. 12:10)."[1]

In consideration of such vile and wicked practices of both the devil and his evil angels, Gifford is going to direct you, the reader, to resist such assaults and submit yourself before God as the weapon of steadfast faith is explained. His text is a famous one, "Be sober and watch: for your adversary the devil, as a roaring lion walketh about, seeking whom he may devour: whom resist steadfast in the faith," (1 Peter 5:8-9). Gifford will show how the Apostle Peter, 1) begins with an admonition or exhortation by which he stirs up all the faithful to sobriety and watchfulness with these words, "Be sober and watch," 2) why it is important to move all men into this position of sobriety and watchfulness, seeing they have such a terrible and cruel adversary who continually seeks their eternal misery and destruction, "For your adversary the devil, as a roaring lion walketh about, seeking whom he may devour." And, 3) teaching how Christians shall withstand him, overcome him, and put him to flight, so that they may escape from his cruel tyranny, "Whom resist steadfast in the faith."

This is an exceedingly helpful work, that will arm the Christian in due manner to fight steadfastly in the power of Jesus Christ through his Spirit against the works and wiles of the devil. And Gifford will not only

---

[1] Wilson, Thomas, *A Complete Christian Dictionary*, (London: E. Cotes, 1661), 159.

show how to do this, but how to do it *effectively*, with victory, through true Christian faith empowered by God's Christ.

In the Savior's Grace and Power,
C. Matthew McMahon, Ph.D., Th.D.
From my study, September, 2020.

Meet George Gifford
Edited by C. Matthew McMahon, Ph.D., Th.D.

George Gifford (1547-1620) was a most excellent puritan divine educated in Hart-hall, Oxford, where he continued for a number of years. In 1582 he became vicar of Maldon in Essex.[2] The *Oxford Historian* describes him as "a very noted preacher, a man admirably well versed in the various branches of good literature, and a great enemy to popery."[3] Mr. Strype says, "he was a great and diligent preacher, and much esteemed by many people of rank. By his labors he brought the town to much more sobriety and knowledge of true religion."[4] He was a decided puritan, and scrupled conformity in various particulars. He wrote with great zeal against the Brownists, and in defense of the church. But all these things were mere trifles, so long as he did not admire the ceremonies, nor come up to the standard of conformity required by the prelates. Therefore, having preached the doctrine of *limited obedience to the civil magistrate*, complaints were brought against him, and he was immediately suspended and cast into prison. This was in the year 1584.

About the same time, this learned divine, and twenty-seven other ministers of Essex, presented a supplication to the lords of the council. The ministers

---

[2] Fuller's *Hist. of Cam.* p. 75.
[3] Wilkins on *Preaching*, p. 83.
[4] Palmer's *Noncon. Mem.* vol. ii. p. 38.

Meet George Gifford

who subscribed to this supplication were highly celebrated for learning, piety, and usefulness, many of whom were already suspended for nonconformity. In the supplication they express themselves as follows. "We cheerfully and boldly offer this our humble suit unto your honors, being our only sanctuary upon earth, next to her majesty, to which we can repair in our present necessity. And most of all we are encouraged, when we consider how richly God has adorned your honors with knowledge, wisdom, and zeal for the gospel, and with godly care and tender love to those who profess the same. Most humbly, therefore, we beseech your honors, with your accustomed favor in all godly and just causes, to hear and to judge of our matters. We have received the charge of her majesty's loyal and faithful subjects, to instruct and teach our people in the way of life; and every one of us having this sounded from the God of heaven, *Woe be unto me, if I preach not the gospel*, we have all endeavored to discharge our duties, and to approve ourselves both to God and men. Notwithstanding this, we are in great heaviness, and some of us already put to silence, and the rest living in fear; not that we have been, or can be charged, we hope, with false doctrine, or slanderous life; but because we refuse to subscribe that there is nothing contained in the *Book of Common Prayer* contrary to the word of God.[5] We do protest in the sight of God, who searches all hearts, that we do not refuse from a desire to dissent, or

---

[5] Strype's *Aylmer*, p. 110.

from any sinister affection; soliciting a redress of their thought it does not bear out in the fear of God, and from the necessity of conscience. The apostle teaches, that a person who doubts is "condemned if he eat."[6] If a man then be condemned for doing a lawful action, because he doubts whether it be lawful; how much more should we incur the displeasure of the Lord, and justly deserve his wrath, if we should subscribe, being fully persuaded that there are some things in the book contrary to his word? If our reasons might be so answered by the doctrine of the Bible, and we could be persuaded that we might subscribe lawfully, and in the fear of God, we would willingly consent. In these and other respects we humbly crave your honorable protection, as those who from the heart do entirely love, honor, and obey her excellent majesty and your honors, in the Lord. Giving most hearty thanks to God for all the blessings we have received from him, by your government, constantly praying, night and day, that he will bless and preserve her majesty and your honors to eternal salvation.[7]

> Your honors poor and humble supplicants,
> George Gifford, Samuel Cotesford, Richard Rogers, Richard Illison, Nicholas Colpotts, William Serdge, Lawrance Newman, Edmund Barker, William Dike, Richard Blackwell, Thomas Chaplain, Thomas Howell, Arthur Dent,

---

[6] MS. *Register*, p. 330.
[7] Strype's *Whitgif.* p. 158.

Meet George Gifford

Mark Wirsdale, Thomas Redrich, Robert Edmonds, Giles Whiting, Augustine Pigot, Ralph Hawden, Camiulus Rusticus, Jeffery Jesselin, John Jiuckle, Thomas Upcue, Thomas Carew, Roger Carr, John Bishop, John Wilton."[8]

When Mr. Gilford was brought to trial before the high commission, his enemies utterly failed in their evidence, and he was accordingly released. This, however, was not the end of his troubles. He did not enjoy his liberty for very long. Bishop Aylmer appointed spies to watch him, and fresh complaints were soon brought against him on account of his nonconformity. Again he was suspended and cast into prison.[9] On this he made application to the lord treasurer, who endeavored to obtain the favor of the archbishop; but his grace having consulted his brother of London, told the treasurer that he was a ringleader of the nonconformists; that he himself had received complaints against him, and was determined to bring him before the high commission.[10]

Mr. Gifford had many friends, and was greatly beloved by his numerous hearers. The parishioners of Maldon, therefore, presented a petition to the bishop, in behalf of their minister, signed by fifty-two people, two of whom were bailiffs of the town, two justices of the

---

[8] Neal's *Puritans*, vol. 1, p. 379.
[9] Strype's *Whitgift*, p. 159.
[10] Strype's *Aylmer*, pp. 111-112.

peace, four aldermen, fifteen head burgesses, and other respectable people. In this petition, they showed that his former accusations had been proved to be false; that the present charges were only the slanderous accusations of wicked men, who sought to injure his reputation and usefulness; that they themselves and a great part of the town had derived the greatest benefit from his ministry; that his doctrine was always sound and good; that in all his preaching and catechizing he taught obedience to magistrates; that he used no conventicles; and that his life was modest, discreet, and unreprovable. For these reasons they earnestly entreated his grace in restoring him to his ministry.[11] Indeed, the distresses of the people in Essex were at this time so great, that the inhabitants of Maldon and the surrounding country presented a petition to parliament for the removal of present grievances. In this petition, now before me, they complain, in most affecting language, that nearly all their learned and useful ministers were forbidden to preach, or deprived of their livings; and that ignorant and wicked ministers were put in their places.

    These endeavors proved ineffectual. Mr. Gifford did not enjoy his liberty for several years, as appears from a supplication of several of the suspended ministers in Essex, presented to parliament, dated March 8, 1587, when he was still under the episcopal censure. It will be proper to give the substance of it in their own words. "In most humble and reverent duty to this high and

---

[11] *MS. Register*, p. 748.

honorable court of parliament, sundry of the ministers and preachers of God's holy word in the county of Essex, present this our earnest supplication, and lamentable complaint, beseeching you upon our knees for the Lord's sake, and the sake of his people, whose salvation it concerns, to bow down a gracious ear to this our most dutiful suit, and to take such order as to your godly wisdom shall be thought most convenient. Your humble suppliants having, by the goodness of God, conducted themselves at all times, both in their doctrine and life, as becomes their vocation, they submit themselves to any trial and punishment, if it should be found otherwise. Notwithstanding this, they have been a long time, and still are, grievously troubled and molested; of which troubles this is one of the heaviest, that we are hindered from the service of God in our public ministry. To this restraint we have hitherto yielded and kept silence."

He continues, "We hoped, from the equity of our cause, the means that have been used, and the necessities of our people, that our suspension would have been taken off by those whose censure lieth upon us. But they neither restored us to our ministry, nor furnished the people with suitable persons to suitors to them, desiring him we might be restored to our former service and usefulness among them; and, notwithstanding our cause has been recommended to them by some of the chief nobility in the land, even of her majesty in her honorable privy council, we have obtained no relief for ourselves, nor comfort for our distressed people. Therefore, to appear before this high and honorable court of parliament, is the only means left to us; that if there be in us no desert of so heavy a sentence, it may please this high court to take such order for the relief of your most humble suppliants as to your godly wisdom shall be thought convenient."

"We, indeed, acknowledge that diverse causes of our restraint are alleged against us; but our earnest desire is, that this high court would by some means be informed of this weighty matter. The chief of them is our refusing to subscribe to certain articles relating to the present policy of the church, that every word and ceremony appointed to be read and used in the *Book of Common Prayer*, is according to the word of God. We declared that we could not, with a good conscience, subscribe to all that was required of us; and we humbly requested to have our doubts removed, and to be satisfied in the things required; but we have not received one word of answer to this day; and their former rigorous proceedings have not in the least been mitigated."

"We humbly pray this high court to be assured of our dutiful obedience to all lawful authority, unto which, as we and our people have been humble to the ordinance of God, and for conscience sake, with all our hearts, we promise and protest our submission. We seek unto you to obtain some relief for us. And we commit our lives and whole estate to Almighty God, to your gracious clemency, and to the care of her right excellent majesty, ceasing not, day and night, to pray that the blessings of grace and glory may rest upon you forever."

This supplication was signed by George Gifford, Ralph Hawden, William Tunstall, John Huckle, Giles Whiting, and Roger Carr; but whether it proved of any advantage, is extremely doubtful. Most probably they continued much longer under suspension. He lived to a good old age, and died about the year 1620.

His works (which Puritan Publications is currently working to republish) are:
1. Country Divinity, containing a Discourse of certain points of Religion among the Common sort of Christians, with a plain Confutation thereof, 1581.
2. A Sermon on the Parable of the Sower, 1581.
3. A Dialogue between a Papist and a Protestant, applied to the capacity of the Unlearned, 1583.
4. Against the Priesthood and sacrifice of the Church of Rome, in which you may perceive their Impiety in usurping that Office and Action which ever appertained to Christ only, 1584.
5. A Sermon on 2 Peter 1:11, 1584.
6. A Catechism, giving a most excellent light to those that seek to enter the Path-way to Salvation, 1580.
7. A Sermon on James 2:14-26, 1586.
8. A Discourse of the subtle Practices of Devils by Witches and Sorcerers, 1587.
9. Sermons on the first four Chapters and part of the fifth chapter of Ecclesiastes, 1589.

10. A short Treatise against the Donatists of England, whom we call Brownists, in which, by Answer unto their Writings, their Heresies are noted, 1590.

11. A Plain Declaration that our Brownists be full Donatists, by comparing them together from point to point out of the writings of Augustine, 1591.

12. A Reply to Mr. Job. Greenwood and Henry Barrow, touching on "read prayer," in which their gross Ignorance is detected, 1591.

13. A Sermon at Paul's Cross, on Psalm 133, 1591.

14. A Dialogue concerning Witches and Witchcrafts; in which is laid open how craftily the Devil deceiveth not only the Witches, but others, 1593.

15. A Treatise of True Fortitude, 1594.

16. A Commentary or Sermons on the whole Book of Revelation, 1596.

17. Two Sermons on 1 Peter 5:8-9, 1598.

18. Four Sermons upon several parts of Scripture, 1598.[12]

19. An Exposition on the Song of Solomon, 1612.

20. Five Sermons on the Song of Solomon, 1620.

21. An English Translation of Dr. Fulke's Prelections on the Holy Revelations.

---

[12] Four Sermons Upon Several Parts of Scripture by George Gifford preacher of the word, at Maudlin in Essex. (London. Thomas Judson, 1598), which was the original title of this current volume.

Preface

To the Right Worshipful Mr. Joseph Bainham Esquire, and to Mistress Joan Bainham his wife.

Sir,

I call to mind the reverent and holy memory of that godly martyr both of your name, country, and house, Mr. James Bainham, who died most constantly for the truth of the Gospel, as we have his story at large described in Mr. Fox.[13] I consider with his death the great mercy of God, in continuing still to that worshipful name and stock, the same light of faith, and zeal of the truth, and holiness of profession. I do not doubt to say to you, as the holy Apostle wrote to Timothy, "When I call to remembrance the unfeigned faith that is in thee, which dwelt first in thy grandmother Lois, and in thy Mother Eunice, and am assured that it dwelleth in thee also," (2 Tim. 1:5). So it cannot be but a great joy and comfort to those that fear God, to see the posterity of martyrs, to still retain the holy faith and profession of the martyrs. Not only to be of their earthly linage, but also of their spiritual kindred. Not to be next to them only in generation, but to follow them in regeneration. And your example, as it is to us an occasion of rejoicing, so to you it must serve, not as a

---

[13] Fox's *Book of Martyrs*, page 1030.

spur to prick you, but as a star to direct you, and a line to lead and draw you forward to all holy increase of faith and zeal.

That holy man, as he was virtuous in his life, devout in prayer, sound in faith, patient in his afflictions; so, most of all was he constant and cheerful in his death. He, in the midst of his torments, and out of the raging flames of fire, in this way spoke with a comfortable and heavenly voice: "O you Papists, behold, you look for miracles, and here now you may see a miracle, for in this fire I feel no more pain, then if I were in a bed of goose-down." But it is to me as sweet as a bed of roses.

How we ought now, to honor the memory of this blessed man, and how much are you to praise God, that has given you out of your worshipful house so worthy an example and encouragement to all Christian proceeding? I say again with the same Apostle, "Wherefore I put you in remembrance that you stir up the gift of God in you," *etc.* (2 Timothy 1:6). And I do not doubt, but that as it is true generally in the church, *Sanguis Martyrum semen Ecclesiae*, "the blood of the martyrs is the seed of the Church," so more especially in your family, that it has been blessed of God, and made fruitful, being seasoned as it were by the blood of so holy a man. Saint Ambrose says, *Passio Christi sufficit ad salutem, passio Martyrum contulit ad exemplum,* "Christ's death is sufficient to salvation, and the martyr's death is effectual for an example and instruction." You have both Christ's holy passion to save you, and this martyr's worthy example and confession to instruct you. The memory of this excellent man gave me occasion to present this sermon to you, which came to my hands, which contains a profession of the same faith for the which he died, in you reverencing his remembrance, and honoring his faith. May God grant us all the same zeal and holiness in our lives, that we may have the same comfort and cheerfulness in our end.

Your Worship's one who wishes you well in the Lord,
THOMAS MAN

Resist Steadfast in the Faith[14]

"Be sober and watch: for your adversary the devil, as a roaring lion walketh about, seeking whom he may devour: whom resist steadfast in the faith," (1 Peter 5:8-9).

Peter, an apostle of Jesus Christ (1 Peter 1:1), wrote this epistle to the Christian Jews who lived as strangers dispersed throughout various countries like Pontus, Galatia, Cappadocia, Asia, and Bithynia. The ten tribes had been scattered since ancient times, dwelling for centuries among the Gentiles in many different kingdoms, having been carried away by Shalmaneser, King of Ashur, out of their own land (2 Kings 17). Sometime later, many of the tribes of Judah and Benjamin were also dispersed among the heathen. For this reason, James wrote his epistle in the same manner to the twelve tribes which were in the *dispersion* (James 1:1). These dispersed Jews came up from various lands to Jerusalem at certain solemn feast times in order to worship there according to the law of Moses. There they heard the apostles preach Christ and many believed in him (Acts 2). And it was to those that believed that James and Peter directed their epistles.

---

[14] Two sermons on 1 Peter 5:8-9, in which is shown that the devil is to be resisted only by a steadfast faith, however he comes either against soul or body. And that for whoever has once attained the true and lively faith, it can never be utterly lost, but he is sure to gain the victory.

Concerning the matters handled in this epistle of Peter, we note that the holy apostle deals primarily with the *duties* of the Christian life. And as the times then were full of troubles and terrors of persecutions, he urges them to be bold, patient, constant and cheerful in all afflictions and sufferings which they were to pass through in order to partake of the heavenly glory with Christ. He also uses many grave and forcible reasons to move them to true holiness, to walk in the virtues of the Spirit of grace, and to bring forth fruits worthy of so high a calling.

But first of all, he opens as it were the fountain and beginning of all good actions in man, that is, how God in his great mercy chose them and begot them in Christ to be his children and heirs of glory. Among these various persuasions, admonitions and exhortations of the apostle, the one I have quoted to you in the beginning I will now discuss.

It may be divided into three parts: 1) He begins with an admonition or exhortation by which he stirs up all the faithful to sobriety and watchfulness with these words, "Be sober and watch." 2) He shows why it is important to move all men into this position of sobriety and watchfulness, seeing they have such a terrible and cruel adversary who continually seeks their eternal woe and destruction, "For your adversary the devil, as a roaring lion walketh about, seeking whom he may devour." 3) He teaches how we shall withstand him, overcome him, and put him to flight, so that we may escape from his cruel tyranny, "Whom resist steadfast in the faith."

All men may easily see that the matter we are dealing with here is of *great importance.* If a man has lands or goods and perceives that he has an adversary lying in wait, seeking to deprive him of the same, he will be moved to take heed. He will be motivated to seek out all the ways and means he can to learn how he can defend himself and his lands and goods and hold onto what is rightfully his. If a man knows his enemy is continually seeking all opportunities and all occasions and all advantages, coming to take away his life, will he not watch and take heed? He would certainly be glad to learn how he might arm and strengthen himself so that he can withstand this enemy when he attacks. And yet this is a far greater matter, as it is not the loss of goods or lands, or even of this frail life, but the destruction of both body and soul in eternal damnation, which is sought by a very mighty, subtle, and cruel enemy. I know therefore that those with any spark of true wisdom will be very attentive to hearken to this exhortation of the apostle, desirous to learn how they may be kept safe from so great a danger.

For how foolish is it to be watchful of men who may wish to harm us (though it is in lighter matters) while forgetting that there are devils which seek our eternal woe and misery? Take heed, therefore beloved, to this wholesome instruction: for now, I will deal with each aspect separately.

1) "Be sober and watch." Watching that we may keep ourselves out of danger is the chief and principal matter of this exhortation. And because no man is fit to watch unless he is sober, he joins them both together, and says to us, "Be sober and watch." It is a vain practice to call drunken men to watch, for sleep will soon oppress them. But he that is sober may watch; so be sober, therefore, (the apostle says) and watch.

For our further instruction in this point, let us remember that there are two kinds of drunkenness, two kinds of soberness, two sorts of sleeping, and two sorts of watching. The one is of the body, the other of the mind. When a man takes in excessive amounts of wine and strong drink until he is drunk and his senses are suppressed, drowsiness comes over him and he falls into a sound sleep. When he is in this state, his adversary may attack him and do what he will to him. He that keeps himself sober and does not allow himself to be overcome with wine or strong drink, but uses them moderately, he can watch in order to ward off and withstand perils and dangers.

As the body is made drunk with wine or strong drink, so the mind can be oppressed and made drunk with earthly cares, carnal pleasures, evil lusts, and vain delights. These cause the mind to become drowsy and fall into a dead sleep, so that the spiritual enemy may attack him and do to him what he will. On the contrary, he that keeps his mind sober regarding those cares and pleasures, so that he is not oppressed nor drowned in them, he can watch in order that he may avoid spiritual dangers. This is what Peter is exhorting us to do here, that we cast cares and vain pleasures out of our mind, so that in times of extreme peril we may continue sober and fit to watch against all spiritual dangers. Our Savior Christ teaches that the heavenly seed is choked with cares and pleasures of this life (Luke 8:14). And many may wonder whether Peter is speaking only to that sobriety of the mind, or is it his purpose to exhort to sobriety in drinking also, together with that of the mind? I answer that he requires both: inasmuch as a man cannot have a sober and watchful mind who tends to be given to drunkenness. For those who are given to gluttony and drunkenness, or who take pleasure in pampering the flesh, their mind is drowned in all sorts of lusts and carnal pleasures and cares of earthly matters. They are concerned with how they may provide for the filling of those insatiable lusts. Their mind is also drunken and in a dead sleep, so that they cannot watch in order to ward off any spiritual danger. This is the extreme misery of those who are consumed with vain delights: they are drunken and asleep, so the devil may put into them almost *anything* he wills. And therefore, our Savior Christ warns his disciples to watch for his coming to judgment, charging them first to beware lest at any time their hearts should be oppressed with gluttony and drunkenness and the cares of this life and that day come suddenly upon them (Luke 21:34-36).

Here we see plainly that our Savior joins both the bodily drunkenness and the drunkenness of the mind together, and this combination makes men utterly unfit to watch. Beloved, let us give good heed and follow this wise counsel which the Holy Spirit gives us by this apostle. For if we do not watch, we will be utterly undone, we are utterly cast away, as is made evident by the next words. We cannot watch unless we keep our minds from the drunkenness of cares and carnal pleasures, and our bodies from excess of wine and strong drink and continue sober.

2) "For your adversary the devil, as a roaring lion walketh about, seeking whom he may devour." If we are not senseless, careless, and void of all concerns, and if we are not like mad men, then this warning should move us to be sober and watchful in mind and body for there is a fearful and horrible danger set before us. If we do not watch, our cruel enemy the devil roams about, continually seeking opportunity to greedily devour our souls, yes, even to swallow us up to eternal damnation in hell.

Is it a light matter, beloved, to be devoured of the devil? Is it nothing to go to hell? If we do not watch, we are sure to fall into his hands. We are sure to be devoured and swallowed up into the horrible gulf of hell if we do not learn to be sober and to watch, in order that we may avoid him. For if we are drunken and asleep in our mind, he comes on us, and there is no help nor any way to escape him.

Behold what worldly cares and pleasures of the flesh bring men to, which is to say that they cannot watch, but their mind is drowned and cast into a deep sleep, so that the devil comes on them and takes them as prey, swallowing them up to eternal captivity. But there is great force in every word to express to us this danger, and therefore, I will handle these particularly.

Your adversary. Peter shows us our adversary; and what do men look for at the hands of a deadly adversary, but all the harm and mischief that he can do to them. Therefore, each man has an eye on his adversary, to beware of him, so that he does not catch him at any advantage.

This adversary burns in such extreme hatred and malice against God and all mankind that his name in Hebrew is *Satan*, which means "adversary," because he is the chief of all adversaries. There is no way to seek reconciliation with him, there is no truce to be made, nor any mitigation of his cruel fury to be looked for. But we may be sure of all the mischief and harm that he can do to us, be sure of that. There is no pity or mercy with him, neither is he in any way to be trusted, for he is a liar, he is a deceiver, he is a devil. Your adversary *the devil.* As he is called Satan in the Hebrew tongue, in the Greek tongue his name is *Diabolos*, which we call devil, meaning one who accuses, depraves, and lays blame for crimes. He is nothing but falsehood and lies; there is no trusting and no hope of mitigation for his cruel rage. But it may be questioned, seeing the multitudes of nations and people upon the earth are so many, how can one devil put all these in danger? Peter speaks of one devil. While he is in one country, he cannot be in another, and while he is dealing with one man, another then goes free.

It is true that Peter speaks of only one devil, not because he is just one. For the holy scriptures teach that there are multitudes, as it were, armies of devils which encompass us about, seeking our utter destruction. We read about a legion of devils (demons) in the gospels which possessed one man; as it is said, they *were many*. But Peter here speaks of one, because there is but one kingdom of Satan, and one prince of darkness, and that kingdom is not divided. Satan is not divided against Satan, as our Savior teaches (Matthew 12). They all deal in one busines, one does not envy another, one does not hinder another, but they all further one cause. And so, they join altogether as one devil. The bond which binds them together in this consent is that cruel malice and hatred with which they burn against both God and man. So, if God is dishonored and blasphemed, it pleases them by whomever it is done. As long as men are brought to damnation, they do not care which of them prevails most. If one of them casts a man halfway to perdition, and another finishes the job, they do not argue which of them did the most. There is no need for praise or commendation in that kingdom, as all are driven by a vehement passion for evil. There is no man free then from the assaults and temptations of devils; they seek to devour every soul. Let no man imagine then that he can be lulled to sleep in his mind and remain free from danger. He that will escape must be sober and watch, for a multitude of devils surround us.

It is further said that he is *a roaring lion*. We are very fast asleep if this roaring cannot awake us, and cause us to be sober and watch, especially if we consider why he roars. It is written in Psalm 104:21 that the lions roar after their prey. Being hungry and greedy, they *roar* after their prey. So, to express how greedily Satan hunts after the souls of men, how hungry he is to devour them, he is compared to a roaring lion which seeks his prey. This comparison shows that he is very terrible, for a lion is a mighty beast. The fact that he is hungry and greedy and roars for his prey just increases his terror. The devil is defined here as *mighty*, since he is compared to a roaring lion that is hungry and greedy to devour the souls of men. Who then that is wise will make himself drunken in mind with cares and pleasures, and lie sleeping when such a terrible enemy seeks to devour him?

And now it may be questioned, why does the Holy Spirit describe him as being so mighty and so terrible? Because if we are negligent to keep ourselves sober of mind and body, and allow ourselves to be overwhelmed, drowning in lusts and carnal pleasures as if there were no danger at all, then we are as mad men. Therefore, the Scripture, both here and in other places, describes the devil to be so horrible. Paul calls the devils "empires and powers, the rulers of the darkness of this world, and spiritual wickedness in the high places." He shows that the devils have *fiery darts* with which they seek to pierce through and slay the souls of men (Eph. 6:12-16). What a dreadful monster is he described to be (Rev. 12). He is not only compared to a dragon, but also a great, monstrous dragon from whose mouth flows a flood of waters, and whose tail casts down a third part of the stars of heaven. He is not only a most monstrous great dragon, but also fiery red, burning with hatred, with cruelty, and with blood. Full of deep subtleties, for he has seven heads. He is very mighty, having ten horns. He is shown to have conquered nations of the world, for he has seven crowns. What a terror is set forth in all these – a hungry roaring lion, mighty powers with fiery darts, a monstrous and fierce dragon, full of subtlety, cruelty, and power?

Is there any excuse to be drunken and to sleep? Should we not rather be sober and watching? Most certainly, unless we consider it a small matter to fall prey to the paws of this roaring lion, to have our souls pierced through and wounded to death with his fiery darts and swallowed up into the belly of this dragon, cast into the lake of fire with him and his armies of devils (Rev. 20:14).

Beloved, let us not be so dull hearted and careless when the Lord warns us of such an adversary, as if we had no enemy at all that seeks out our destruction. Men naturally fear and tremble at any signs of the presence of devils. If he showed himself in an ugly form, they would be terrified: and yet most carelessly they make their own minds drunken with cares and carnal pleasures, falling into a dead sleep, so that he utterly ruins them, wounding them to death, even though they do not feel it and are not aware of it.

This is the course of almost the whole world. How many thousand thousands have drunk themselves with the delights of this world, and are then devoured as prey by this roaring lion and swallowed up by the dragon?

Drunken people, especially when they fall into a deep sleep, have no clear understanding of their miseries. Whether they are in debt, or condemned to death, they laugh, and so play with the drunken world. How it is necessary that we are sober and watch to the end that we may escape such dangers? Further, this adversary goes about seeking whom he may *devour*. This greatly increases the peril, which ought to move us to a sure state of sobriety and watchfulness. This adversary continually seeks every occasion and lies in wait to take advantage of every opportunity for how he may devour us as his prey.

If a man has a strong adversary that hates him so fiercely that if he could catch him, he would take away his life, but the same adversary lives in a far-away country and does not lie in wait to catch him at every turn, he may feel more secure, he may sleep quietly. But if he is always at hand, waiting around the corner at every opportunity to do him mischief, does it not stand to reason that if he values his own life, he should keep himself sober and watchful? Shall he drink himself into a stupor and lie down to sleep? The devil, our adversary, is ever at hand. He seeks every occasion for how he may devour us. He is very swift, he is never weary, he needs no food nor sleep, he works day and night for our destruction. When we travail through the day, he observes us; when we lie on our beds in the night, he watches for us. There is no time that we can be free from him. If he cannot prevail at one time, he waits for another. If he cannot overcome a man in one sin, he tries him in another, and most carefully he watches for his best occasions, and then he tempts us strongly.

This adversary uses his instruments to draw and persuade a man to drunkenness, riot, and excess and to spend his time in vain. Woe to that man familiar with sinners who will allure and entice him to evil. When Satan finds such instruments to use to draw a man to sin, he has gained a great advantage. When a man is in a place where he secretly commits some sin, as theft or adultery, and such an occasion is put before him, Satan pushes in hard.

Why should I mention specifics, seeing he has a thousand ways, a thousand occasions, yes, even ten thousand slights of hand and crafty means to use against us? Alas, what shall we do? Our Savior commands us to "watch and pray lest ye enter into temptation," (Matt. 26:41). And as he said to Peter, "Simon, Simon, behold, Satan hath desired to sift you as wheat," (Luke 22.31). So be assured, he has many ways at his disposal to sift us, and to try what is in us. We are taught to pray, "Lead us not into temptation," and this truth shows how necessary a prayer it is. For if the Lord gives scope to this enemy and leaves us to ourselves, he will find a thousand means to utterly destroy us. He will even devour us as his prey, and we shall not perceive it, for in this lies the greatest danger, that he blinds the eyes of the mind, and hardens the heart, when men do not feel that he is working, nor imagine any such thing. He that is sober and watches, realizes when Satan moves in to tempt him. But he may do what he will to those who are drunken and asleep, and they never know it. Now let us come to the third and last part.

3) "Whom resist steadfast in the faith." If a man's adversary is too strong for him, how is he bettered by watching if he is not strong enough to resist him? The typical objection here is that the power of the forces of Satan far exceeds all power of man. Described as mighty and terrible, there is no way for a man to hide himself from them; they will find him out and come upon him. So how is he bettered because he watched? Peter answers that although in our own strength we are nothing to this mighty roaring lion, yet there is a power in which we shall resist him, put him to flight, and overcome him, and be armed against all harms. And that is the power of faith, "Whom resist steadfast in the faith." Do not think it is a strange thing that this power is able to resist him and keep us safe, for it is the power of God. The devil is strong and mighty, but what is he

compared to God? God is above all. His power is infinite; there is no power that can stand against it. He that is steadfast in the faith is armed and stands in the power of God, for faith apprehends the power of God and arms us with it. He that stands in the faith, stands as it were in God, encompassed about and covered with his power. And as it is impossible that Satan should prevail against the power of God, so is it impossible that he should overthrow that man which stands steadfast in the faith: for so long as God cannot be overcome, faith cannot be overcome.

Is not here a most singular comfort and consolation to us in this battle? The devil can never be so mighty, subtle, fierce and raging, that we do not have a stronger rock of defense, a safe tower to fly to. In the invincible power of almighty God, we stand armed with faith. This is what Paul taught where he spoke of the battle which we have with the devil, "My brethren be strong in the Lord and in the power of his might. Put on the whole armor of God, that you may stand against the assaults of the devil. For we wrestle not against blood and flesh, but against rulers, against powers, *etc.* Therefore, take unto yourself the whole armor of God, that you may be able to resist in the evil day, and having finished all things, stand," (Eph. 6:10-1).

Now it is faith that puts on us the whole armor of God and makes us strong in his mighty power. It is faith, as he shows in the same place, by which we shall quench all the fiery darts of the devil. Likewise, John lays out this matter, saying, "Whoever is born of God overcomes the world and this is the victory that overcomes the world, even our faith. Who is it that overcomes the world, but he that believes that Jesus is the Son of God?" (1 John 5:4-6). By the "world" he means the whole corruption of sin, or whatever is against the commandment of God, and so the devil, the Prince of the world, is included. He that overcomes the world, overcomes the prince of the world, for all the power of Satan's kingdom is in darkness and in sin. When John says that faith is our victory, and that by it we overcome the world, he teaches that it is by this faith that we are armed with the power of God in which we stand safe and overcome the devil.

In this is manifest what a wonderful and precious thing faith is. There is no force that can overcome it. He that has obtained it cannot be poor, unhappy or wretched; all the devils in hell cannot prevail against him. They that trust in the Lord are as Mt. Zion, which cannot be moved, but stand fast forever (Psalm 125:1). If the most excellent thing is to stand steadfast in the faith, then we are above all other things to seek after it, for wisdom teaches us to seek most the best things. Gold, pearls, and precious stones are quite valuable, so men are thrilled when they find them. It is by faith that we put devils to flight and obtain eternal glory. So, shall we not then seek for faith? And once found, shall we not make the case for having found all? For what can a man have more than God? And if we miss it, we have lost all, seeing that without it nothing can defend us from the assaults of the devil.

But when we resist the devil steadfast in the faith, is it so that we have faith in our own power or will? Can we of *ourselves* be steadfast in faith? Or is it an easy matter to obtain a strong faith? Peter indicated no such thing. For goodly things are hard to attain; and faith is the most precious and excellent of all and most hard to come by. It is not in man's will or power to believe steadfastly at his pleasure. But Peter urges all men to seek it where it is to be found. For a strong faith is a rich jewel. But when it comes to this matter, they deprive themselves for the most part, either deeming that they have it or can have it in their own power resting in a vain shadow, not knowing at all the nature of true, living, powerful faith. Or if they do acknowledge it to be the gift of God, *they never seek it through those means which he ordained to work in men and to nourish it in them.* When we are therefore urged to resist the devil steadfast in the faith, we are to give all diligence and use all the ways and means that you have available to increase and strengthen your faith, that you may overcome the devil. If you are diligent in that, you will be happy. And if you do not take that course, then you will be utterly undone, for what way can you then escape the power and tyranny of the roaring lion?

But it may be said that Peter does not show here how men shall come to this steadfast faith. No, for his whole doctrine points in that direction, throughout this whole epistle.

He that will attain to the true, lively, and justifying faith which arms a man with the power of God must first of all know for certainty that he has not so much as a spark of such faith in himself. We are all by nature bound in unbelief and miserable blindness. Many do not know this, and therefore are *content* with a certain image of *dead faith*. The same are utterly seduced, for that faith has no power whatsoever. He that knows this and beholds the depth of calamity he is in will look to God who is the giver of faith. This man desires to know the promises of God which he is to believe, and how he must perform the duties of the Christian life. For true faith works by charity, as Paul says, and cannot be without good works.

He that searches the Scriptures does with all diligence bend his ear to hear the holy Gospel of Jesus Christ preached, feeling therein the power of God to work faith. He cries and calls to God day and night to teach him, to enlighten him, to give him understanding, and to increase his faith. He finds the blessing of God in these means and therefore applies them. God gives faith to the one who rests in this if it is his will. The one who despises such means, not considering how God gives faith, is utterly in error and out of the right way. This is why there are so many commendations of the word of God, and of the lively power that it has to save our souls.

From here we are often called on to give ear to the voice of God and to listen to his counsels.

In this way we shall obtain the holy faith. And he that has faith and feels the power of God in him, if he would have it increase, should consider the abundant kindness of God who has given him so great a gift. He should from the bottom of his heart give all praise and thanks and honor to him for such a great kindness and mercy shown. Moreover, he that will be steadfast in the faith to resist the devil should take heed that he is rich in good works, and that he abstains from committing those vices which nature leads us into. For in the time of trial, in the hour of temptation, or when Satan assaults us, it will shake a man when he looks for evidence of a true faith and finds that he has been fruitless. But if his conscience accuses him not only of a slackness in good works, but also of foul sins committed, then he will cry out that all his former profession of the faith was hypocrisy.

This apostle in the first chapter of his second epistle teaches that if we join virtue with our faith, and with virtue knowledge, and with knowledge temperance, and with temperance patience, and with patience godliness, and with godliness brotherly kindness, and with brotherly kindness love: we shall make our calling and election sure. If we do these things, we shall never fall (2 Peter 1:5-10). We can perceive with assurance whether these things are in us, knowing that God has called us effectually, and that he has chosen us.

In this consists the steadfastness of our faith, when we are sure that God has chosen us in his Son to eternal life. If this assurance of God's love and favor towards us was not attainable, how could he say, "Whom resist steadfast in the faith?" Can there be any steadfast faith without that? I urge you to think well of these things. Use all care and diligence, as well as all the holy means that God has appointed to increase our faith, that being armed thereby, we may resist and overcome our enemy the devil.

But here it may be questioned as to whether the devil is to be resisted only by faith, or by some other means? I answer that Peter tells us the only way by which we are to resist the devil, for we have nothing sufficient to withstand him but faith. True faith is sufficient alone to withstand him, no matter how he seeks to hurt us.

I suppose the reason is evident to all. No power but the power of God alone is sufficient to shield us from the devil. Faith arms us with that power of God and makes it as if it were ours. He that stands and lives by faith, stands and lives not in himself but in the power of God. If we think it is lawful to seek help to resist him, and to put him to flight anywhere but in God, then we may attempt to use some other way to resist him besides faith.

We are to resist him by prayer, some will say. That is true, for prayer is a special fruit of faith, as lively faith brings forth true prayer. If the prayer is not of faith, it cannot help to deliver us from the tyranny of Satan. Faith sends up prayer, and with fasting, strong prayer draws the power of God down on us, which shields and defends us from the rage of the evil one. All other means that have been used to put devils to flight are vain and frivolous, mere illusions of Satan's own devising, which wickedly defaces the power of God. For when men cannot resist by faith, they resort to these other means as surer.

Woeful is the state of the world in this thing, that when men will not learn of God to resist the devil: they learn from the devil himself. But that this may be more evident, we are to see how many ways the devil seeks to devour us. I do not mean that we should see all those ways by which the devil devours the souls of men in particular: for who is able to express them all? Surely not any mortal man. For he has many subtleties and crafts, as many as ten thousand devices of all sorts to snare and trap the souls of man. He also has his forces and fiery darts of terror to wound us all. To be strongly armed to resist him, however he comes to attack, is the aim here. My purpose is simply to touch on some general areas, in which all the rest are contained. This cruel adversary, this roaring lion the devil, is out to catch his prey and devour it; he does not care which way he does it, for the end is to carry souls with him to hell.

It is likely that no man will doubt that the devil desires to plunge all men as deep as he can into all evil. But depending on how a man is inclined, he deals with some one way and with others a different way. Those who are ignorant and in darkness, he keeps the pure, clear, and heavenly light of the Gospel out of their hearts, and so holds them under the power of the kingdom of darkness. Concerning those who Paul said, "If our Gospel be hid, it is hid to those that perish: in whom the God of this world hath blinded their minds, lest the light of the Gospel of the glory of Christ, should shine unto them, which is the image of God," (2 Cor. 4:3-4). The enemy uses special means to bring this to pass, by which he may defame the Gospel and one's profession of faith. Namely, he sows errors, heresies, and wicked opinions about the Gospel. He is the father of all such things. He raises up heretics as his chief servants, and then persuades them to proclaim this heresy as truth. From such comes many foul heresies and divisions. How can this be of God? How can it be good doctrine which brings forth such fruit?

Satan practiced this while the holy apostles were alive on the earth. We read how the false apostles sought almost everywhere to discount and destroy what Paul had established as truth. John in Revelation mentions the Nicolaitans, and a woman who said she was a Prophetess, teaching and seducing the servants of the Lord that they might commit fornication and eat meat that had been offered to idols. And the same apostle said that in his time there were many "antichrists," (1 John 2). Paul said to the elders of Ephesus, "I know this, that after my departure there shall enter in among you grievous wolves, not sparing the flock, and there shall rise up of yourselves that shall speak perverse things to draw disciples after them," (Acts 20).

When all the apostles were gone, this prophecy was fully accomplished, for then the devil sent forth wicked heretics which seduced many in the churches. He planted those who preached, "Behold what a Gospel that produces such foul and monstrous opinions." Satan craftily worked these cunning lies to keep many bound by their former blindness. And in the same way today, when the light of the Gospel breaks forth, he raises up horrible heresies and sects to lead many astray. This offends many, so that even though they hear the true Gospel, the devil holds them in their former blindness and devours them as prey. He also raises up lies and slanders to defame both the doctrine and all that profess it. This has been his ancient practice. Christ was said to have a devil, to be a raiser of sedition, and an enemy to Caesar. His apostles were deemed to be raisers of factions and disturbers of the common peace, enemies to the state of princes, and the Christians were accused of being men who secretly among themselves committed foul and abominable sins. It is true that throughout all times there have been hypocrites that profess the truth for a time and then fall into notorious offences, but all the professors were said to be such. In this way and in all times Satan has held many in darkness. When Christ was raised from the dead, Satan spread a lie that while the watchmen were asleep, the disciples of Christ stole him away, and then said he was risen. And this lie was believed (though it was absurd with no evidence of likelihood).

See what lies and slanders he creates no so that many believe. For as Paul said in 2 Thessalonians 2, "Because men receive not the love of the truth, God sends them strong delusion to believe lies." For a man to resist the devil in these practices, he cannot be seduced and held in blindness. It is necessary to have knowledge of the truth and a lively faith. For if he comes once to that, he shall find that the Gospel is the pure and heavenly light, even the power of God to salvation as Paul says, "to everyone that believeth," (Rom. 1:16). These sects and heresies and troubles that follow it are raised up by the devil himself, to defame the truth, so that men may despise it when they hear it preached. Such as have received the knowledge of the truth and are enlightened, in them he seeks how he may quench the light or take the power of it out of their hearts, and so devour them as his prey.

He has many ways and means to affect this. To those who are weak in knowledge, and for those who are babes in their understanding of the heavenly mysteries, he lays stumbling blocks and offences that he may cause them to stumble and fall or to turn aside out of the way into which they have entered. He raises up terrors, troubles, and perils to destroy them. He tempts and leads men to despair. The only way to avoid these perils, and what Paul prayed for the faithful at Colossae, is to be "filled with the knowledge of the will of God in all wisdom and spiritual understanding: that we may walk worthy of the Lord in all pleasing, being fruitful in all good works, and increasing in the knowledge of God: strengthened in all might through his glorious power, unto all patience and long suffering with joyfulness," (Col. 1:9-11). Others that have received more knowledge he seeks to destroy through pride and presumption. He leads them into sects, errors, and heresies, as his occasion serves, one part into one, another into another.

This is why there is such a need for sound knowledge of heavenly things and of that sincere faith which purges the heart and empties it of pride and presumption, leading men to rest only on God with fear and trembling and true humility. He also tempts and leads men into grievous and abominable sins according to their inclinations, and in this way destroys them. He is utterly subtle and can find what sin a man most easily can be led into.

If he is inclined to vain amusements and lusts, he finds friends who are inclined to the same, so that when he experiences spiritual or heavenly notions, they are quenched by desires for such amusement with friends. If he is inclined to unclean lusts of fornication, he will find the means to set the bait before him so that he may be enticed. And so is it in all other vices: so that men must *watch and pray lest they enter into temptation.* They need to be armed with a steadfast faith to resist, that by their faith all the fiery darts of this horrible enemy may be quenched. Because of his ability to keep men in blindness, his lies and slanders that drive men from the Gospel, his assaults that lead men into despair, his stumbling blocks and terrors to turn men out of the way, his temptation to lead into heresies and sects or into any foul sin, or whatever darts he shoots, the only way to be kept safe from his fiery darts is to possess a true, a lively, and a steadfast faith.

Therefore, beloved, seeing this enemy is so vigilant, and so seeks our destruction night and day, even to swallow us up into the gulf of hell, and seeing he has so many traps, baits and allurements to wound to death those he wishes to destroy, having no power of ourselves, let us seek to be strongly armed with the power of God so that we may get the victory. There is no way for us to be armed with the power of God but by faith; so, the end of all this is that men labor to increase and strengthen their faith. Use all the means God makes available to you for the furtherance of the same. If, in light of such a danger we will not be admonished by this wholesome admonition of the apostle, we are either foolish or mad.

Some may say that the devil is to be resisted only by faith when he comes to hurt the soul. But is it not another opportunity when he comes to hurt the body or the possessions of a man? Should he not also then be resisted by faith? Whether he comes to do those things of himself or by witches and sorcerers, there is no other means available to us to resist him but by faith. Granted, the devils delight to torment and to hurt man in any way. We see this plainly taught in the scriptures where he has been granted power on occasion to do harm, as in the case of Job, when he was granted permission by God to destroy Job's goods, to kill his children, and then to plague his body with grievous sores. We read of many in the Gospel whose bodies were possessed with devils, and whom he was allowed to torment in destructive manners.

Further, we must know that when he hurts one's body or possessions, his chief aim is to destroy both body and soul, and so he makes it a means to win the soul. We read in the Gospel of two possessed with devils, and when Jesus cast out the devils, they sought permission from him to enter into a herd of swine. He gave them leave, they entered, and carried the whole herd of swine headlong off a cliff and into the sea and drowned them (Matthew 8). What was the purpose of those devils, what was their desire? Was it no more than to destroy the poor dumb beasts? No, they had a deeper reason, which was to ignite hatred from the men of that region for Christ so that they might not hear the Gospel he was preaching. They knew these men were worldly minded, and that the loss of their hogs would grieve them. And so, the men of that city begged him to leave their coasts. Here was a crafty conveyance of Satan, in which he obtains power to hurt the body of man, his cattle or his goods, because of a greater mischief which he seeks to accomplish. We may be sure that it is all one, whether it comes directly from Satan himself or one of his cohorts. None should be so foolish to imagine that if he has power to harm, that he will lie still and not harm unless he is sent by some man or woman. But unless he has permission granted him from God, no mortal creature can give him power to touch the body or goods of a man. For this reason, however he comes, we must know it is the Lord God of heaven that has sent him, even as he gave him leave to test Job.

It must follow, therefore, that there is no power sufficient to resist him but *the power of God;* and there is no way to be armed with that power *but by faith.* If there is no way to withstand Satan but by the power of God, and it is through faith alone that man is armed with that power, what other way or means can there be to resist him?

There was a child possessed with a devil. The child's father brought him to the disciples of Christ that they might cast out the devil, but they could not accomplish it. They then brought the child to Jesus, who cast him out. The disciples asked the Lord why they could not cast him out, and he told them it was because of their unbelief. "This kind goes not out but by prayer and fasting," (Matthew 17:21). Where we see the devil tormenting the body, it is to be cast out by a strong faith, accompanied with fasting and prayer. But what if when the devil afflicts the body or destroys the goods of a man that it cannot be removed by faith or withstood, shall men then seek to remove him or to withstand him in some other way? We have seen that when the devil possesses and torments the body of some man, woman or child, prayer has been used and yet no remedy has been found. But then he is expelled by some other means. Yes, some believe that God has given Satan power to touch their bodies, their children, or their goods, and they seek God, saying that as he gave him power, so when it pleased him, he would restrain him, and on this truth they would rest. But in the end, they have gladly used *other* means. God has appointed a means, and they who refuse them tempt God.

    If a man falls into a ditch, and lies there praying, "God help me, Lord help me," and does not try to climb out, he may be there for a while. If there are means by which the devil is driven out, why should men not use them, seeing we may suppose that God has appointed those means? In response, we may first consider that to test our faith and patience, the Lord gives leave to Satan to afflict his children. This is for their good. What more proof do we need of this than Job? He was thoroughly tested. Now seeing it was the will of God that he should be tested in this way, both for his own good and for the instruction of many others, though his faith was a right strong faith, it did not repel Satan nor prevent him from having power to touch his goods, his children, and his body. And so, we may know undoubtedly, that if God gives power or permission to Satan to touch the body, the children, or the goods of any faithful man, for such a purpose as he did for Job, faith does not remove him from being afflicted. But he cannot prevail against those who resist him with a strong faith without God's permission. And that is enough for us. Such a man is to submit himself to the chastisement of God for his testing. If Satan cannot be removed from hurting him in those outward things which are of lesser value, let him believe that he can resist him by faith, so that he does not win his soul. The Lord God will in his good time deliver him from the other calamities.

The woman of Canaan in Matthew 15 was a woman who possessed a wonderful faith, for Christ said of her, "I have not found so great faith in Israel," and yet the devil tormented her daughter. She did not seek any other means, but sought out Christ, and asked him to cast out the devil which was so grievously tormenting her child. This was for her trial, and she did for the time endure it, resisting the devil mightily by faith that he could not prevail against her soul.

Moreover, the devil has power given him to afflict some, to plague them in their bodies or in their goods, because of their sins. They have despised the laws of God; they are careless regarding the way of salvation. When this scourge is on them, they should consider how grievously they have offended, and how much they have provoked the Lord to wrath, who has allowed this wicked enemy to plague them. They should now seek the Lord and entreat him to have mercy on them. They should lament and be sorry for their sins and turn from their wicked ways to the way of righteousness. Then this calamity should bring them nearer to God and to the salvation of their souls. They may entreat the Lord on their repentance to remove the plague from them. And if it is not removed, they ought to fast and pray. They should use all good means to come to the true knowledge of God and to a sound faith, that they may escape from being devoured by this enemy to eternal damnation. But if the Lord does not deliver them in time, and they are tormented in their own bodies, or in their children or goods, let them know it is because they have not thoroughly repented or thoroughly sought the Lord as they ought. Let them therefore yet humble themselves further and seek more earnestly to know the way of God, and to be armed with true and lively faith.

There was a woman which had a spirit of infirmity eighteen years. For this reason, she could by no means lift herself up. Jesus healed her and said that Satan had bound her eighteen years (Luke 13:11-15). If the Lord gives Satan power to afflict for such a long time, let us not fall from God, but look to him. Let us not seek to resist Satan in any way but by faith.

You may say it is known by experience that where the devil has tormented some, prayer and all holy means have been used and yet no help has come until other means have been sought. You may think then that there are stronger means available to resist the devil than faith and prayer or some power mightier against him than the power of God. Those means which some men resort to when they cannot prevail by faith are oftentimes prescribed to them by some wise man or woman. These are very trivial things and yet they are more sought than faith, which arms us with the power of God. What a dishonor this is to the high Majesty of the Almighty? What infidelity this is! Shall men run to the devil for help? Is he more able to teach them or does he possess more power than God?

But when the thing is accomplished by means which could not otherwise be obtained, Satan is dismissed, and comfort follows. Does this mean that Satan has dismissed Satan? Has the devil become so foolish that he will hinder his own kingdom? And are men so foolish as to believe that he is driven out by such things?

A man who is tormented in his body may be advised by his neighbors to send for some cunning man. Word is sent back to have him do such and such a thing, and he shall have relief. So, he does that thing, and he has relief. Do we then think that the devil is driven out? No! Rather he ceases from tormenting the body for a time, that he may enter deeper into the soul. He wins by this driving out. Men may be instructed on how to resist him, as offering some burnt offering to him, and so he presents himself no more. It appears that there is a power above faith that puts him to flight. And even some have been of a mind to seek no other ways or means but God to resist or restrain him, but in the end have been glad to use other means. It is lamentable that the faith of any should fail to such a degree, that instead of approaching God with strong repentance, they have turned to the counsel of the devil. If they could not find help by prayer, they might be assured that the Lord would afflict them further, and that with all humbleness they ought to submit themselves under his mighty hand. They should have considered the weakness of their faith, and the grievousness of their sins, and sought by all means possible to gain a steadfast faith and true repentance. Then their affliction by Satan would have been a warning to them, to make them cleave more firmly to God. You may add that God has appointed means, and he that refuses these means tempts God. As an example, should a man cry, "Lord help me," and not be moved? Indeed, if you could prove that God had appointed such means to drive away devils where faith cannot, your saying would be true. But where can you prove in the whole word of God that such means are appointed to put devils to flight? If those means are not given in the holy Scriptures, they are not ordained of God, they are not of faith, and it is not the power of God that expels Satan, but his own craftiness makes him appear to be vanquished when he is not. These are means of his own devising.

    The holy Scriptures condemn this as a most wicked thing, that men should have any dealings with devils. We are to be taught *of God.* Christ Jesus is our *only* physician. If a man is taken lame and suspects that he is bewitched, he may send for some cunning man who prescribes what the lame man should do for healing.

This is all done by direction of the devil and not means appointed by God.

This is unlike the Canaanite woman who came to Christ to have the devil driven out of her daughter and by the strength of her faith would not be denied (Matthew 15). This is more akin to king Saul, who receiving no answer from God, gave in to a witch. Not finding help by faith and prayer, or through other ways that God had appointed, he began to listen to the devil who told him that if he would do such and such a thing, the devil would depart.

But is this not the ultimate trick of Satan when he can set himself up as a teacher so that men learn of him, thinking that they are learning of God? Men may say that we are just glad to have ease, and to find that the devil is expelled, believing that God allowed it. Shall a man be glad to buy ease at such a great price? May we call that ease, when the devil ceases to torment the body for a time, to the end that he may torment both soul and body in hell forever?

If a man is sick from a burning disease, and he takes something to cool the heat temporarily but afterward this causes more burning, is this a good remedy? Is it a good remedy if it comforts for a time, only to worsen the disease afterwards? And yet blind men imagine that Satan is expelled by those means, when in truth he is entering more deeply into their souls.

Tell me this, where does the kingdom of the devil consist? Is he not called the prince of this world and the prince of darkness? In this way, his kingdom consists in infidelity, in darkness, and in sin. He that is under the power of sin, so that sin has dominion over him, is under the power and working of Satan. Sin is his kingdom, sin is his throne, and you cannot separate them. He cannot be expelled where sin remains in force. If pride, envy, covetousness, hatred, malice, self-love, fornication, or any other sin reigns and rules in the heart of man, there rules the devil also, for these are the works of the devil.

Christ said to the Jews, "You are of your father the devil; you do the works of your father," (John 8:44). He that casts out the devil must also cast off those evil works. For he that commits sin is of the devil, as John says in his first epistle, chapter 3. So, is the devil expelled or driven out of that man who still commits sin? I suppose there is no one so void of reason that he would imagine that the devil is driven away from that man in whose heart he has his throne and power. With ignorance of the word and ways of God, you find unbelief. With unbelief, you find the unfruitful works of darkness along with much vanity of mind, profaneness, wicked errors, and abominable vices.

If such a man had some of his cattle destroyed by the devil, he would desire to have the devil expelled, but he does not have faith which arms men with the power of God; he does not have faith which overcomes the world (1 John 5) or which purges the heart (Acts 15) or which quenches the fiery darts of the devil (Eph. 6) or which, as Peter says here, *resists him*. So, he seeks some other means to resist him and to be delivered from him, never considering that he must first have him removed out of his heart.

He should consider that the devil works in the children of disobedience (Eph. 2:2). And therefore, as long as he is disobedient to God, Satan cannot be cast out of his heart. If those thousands of vices which men learn and practice in the world can resist Satan, then it does not matter whether a man is godly or ungodly, faithful or unfaithful in regard to resisting and putting the devils to flight. For if a man's cattle are plagued and destroyed by the devil, and he can deliver the rest if he burns one alive, the Jew or the Turk or the heathen can cast him out as well as the Christian.

As a result, men may be held in infidelity, in blindness and hardness of heart, void of repentance for their sins, because of the craftiness of Satan. For if devils can be put to flight and overcome by such means, then men will never seek to be armed with faith. They will never care for true repentance as long as they can be persuaded that the devil has nothing to do with them. And in this lies one of the greatest tricks of Satan. He devours men when they dream of no peril, because they do not seek to be armed with his mighty power through faith. For when men know there is no way to escape but through faith, they will desire that true faith unless they are mad.

The papists devised many things to drive away devils. Men were persuaded that the sign of the cross put him to flight. They sprinkled conjured holy water on men, and in their houses, in order to keep the devil out. Likewise, if a man had a piece of holy bread in his purse, or anywhere about him, he was considered armed; he could go safely into the darkest night. They had hallowed candles, and within their light the wicked prince of darkness could not approach.

By lightning and thunder and mighty winds, the Lord declares his majesty. But when such tempests arose, the devil gladly convinced men that he had raised them. In this way, he would be seen as a god of power, for he desired to show himself in these tempests and appear with terror.

In order to repel him, the papists used hallowed bells, bells of their saints, which they rang out when any terrible tempest was approaching, trusting that their sound would repel him and put him to flight. And yet Peter did not tell of these; he did not speak of resisting Satan with anything but faith. Such ready means to defend men, and so easy, and yet not one of the apostles mention them. They also say that only through faith do we have victory.

Beloved, you must realize for certain then that all these supposed means are but tricks of the devil which the papists used and still use to this day when they suppose themselves to be cursed. Leave all such ungodly ways which the devil himself promotes, and listen to the Holy Spirit, which helps you resist the devil by being steadfast in the faith. Let all your studies, and work, and concerns be this: to be armed with a strong and lively faith. That alone shall cover and protect you and encompass you about with the almighty power of God. You shall then be as strong as Mount Zion that cannot be removed. All the infernal powers (or as Christ said, "the gates of hell") shall not prevail against you. If you have this faith, the roaring lion shall not devour you. *But all his fiery darts shall be quenched.* He will do what he can to hold you in blindness, to lead you into sin and heresies. He will tempt you to despair, but your faith shall prevail. He will seek to hurt your body and your goods, but armed with this faith you can resist him. Blessed be our Lord that has given us such a *Tower of Refuge.* Amen.

Can One Lose a Steadfast Faith?

"Be sober, be vigilant; because your adversary the devil, as a roaring lion, walketh about, seeking whom he may devour: Whom resist steadfast in the faith, knowing that the same afflictions are accomplished in your brethren that are in the world," (1 Peter 5:8-9).

The Apostle tells us, "Whom resist steadfast in the faith." We have heard the exhortation or warning which Peter gives to all men *to be sober and watch.* We have also seen the reasons it behooves us to be watchful. There is an adversary that seeks to devour both our souls and bodies and send us to eternal destruction. "Your adversary the devil is like a roaring lion, walking about, seeking whom he may devour." We have also learned how to withstand him and get the victory over him, "Whom resist steadfast in the faith" through true faith, which arms a man with the power of God.

The power of God is invincible, capable of gaining the victory over all the terrible might of devils, so that it is impossible for him who has the power of faith to be overcome. It conquers all the infernal powers and triumphs at all times most gloriously over them. It keeps us safe from devils. In this is manifest what a wonderfully rich and precious jewel faith is. Therefore, it should be desired and sought above all other treasures at the hands of God, for he is the giver of it; it is not available through man's own power. Moreover, seeing

God gives it, and nourishes it by means, he that desires to be steadfast in the faith must use those means that God ordained.

It has also been declared that faith is the only thing by which we are able to resist the devil, since faith alone arms us with the glorious power of God. Satan has many ways whereby he seeks to devour and swallow up the souls and bodies of men. He holds some in blindness and ignorance. He leads others into sects, errors, and heresies. He draws men into vices and abominable sins. But no matter what methods he uses, faith in the mighty power of God is sufficient to quench *all* his fiery darts. All other means by which men seek to repel Satan are mere illusions. Men are to be taught of God and not to listen to devils. And yet devils have devised means that some have put into practice, just as the papists did not seek to resist Satan by faith, but invented other ways.

And now it remains as a principal question, spoken plainly, whether any man that has this true and lively faith, by which the devil is resisted, can utterly lose it and fall from God in the end? Can a man's faith utterly fail and be vanquished, so that having resisted Satan for a time steadfast in the faith, yet in the end he may be overcome and devoured by him?

Touching this question, the papists believe that a man may have the true and lively faith and fall from it utterly, allowing this faith to be quenched in him in the end. And so, according to their doctrine, those who stand in this faith and with the same resist the devil, in the end perish eternally.

There are others who differ somewhat from the papish sort about this matter. These believe that the very reprobate are partakers *for a time* of the true, lively, and justifying faith, but then it is wholly and finally extinguished in them. Moreover, they also believe that the same true and lively faith may be wholly extinguished in the elect, but not finally, because it is impossible for the elect to perish. This is where they differ from the papists, which make election conditional. If this doctrine of theirs is true, then no man can be certain of his salvation. There is no man that is sure he shall stand to the end. No man can resist steadfast in the faith. For he that gets victory over the devil by a true and lively faith today, tomorrow may utterly lose his faith and be overcome by the devil. If this is so, then what Peter is teaching us here about the armor of faith must instead be a weapon that can be broken or destroyed or taken from us, leaving us in a very weak position indeed.

This is the thing which we must be sure of, and that shall be made manifest, that whoever possesses this true and lively faith shall undoubtedly gain victory over Satan. Further, it is impossible for his faith to be extinguished; it is impossible for him to perish.

This we affirm, that whoever attains a steadfast faith (the thing which Peter states is essential), that faith can never be overcome. For if it can be overcome, it is not steadfast. Peter's purpose is to teach that so long as a man is steadfast in the faith, so long as he resists the devil and is victorious over him, his faith shall continue to the end. In other words, as many as are steadfast in the faith shall undoubtedly vanquish Satan, and never be vanquished by him. His doctrine shows, then, that although we are encompassed about and beset with devils, who like greedy devouring lions seek continually to swallow us up, if we are armed with a steadfast faith, we can never lose our position and standing in Christ. The devil can never overcome a steadfast faith, so obtain such a faith and you are sure to stand to the end.

Beloved, we are not only to labor for faith, but if we are to overcome the devil and to stand to the end, we must work to obtain a steadfast faith. But how can we be sure that this is the mind of the apostle, to guarantee men that if they possess a steadfast faith, they will surely gain victory over the devil and stay strong to the end? I answer that by saying that here he is agreeing with what he has already taught in the first chapter of his second epistle, "Give all diligence that to your faith you add virtue, to virtue knowledge, to knowledge temperance, to temperance patience, to patience godliness, to godliness brotherly kindness, and to brotherly kindness love. For if these things be among you, and abound, you shall neither be idle nor unfruitful in the knowledge of our lord Jesus Christ. "For he that does not have these things is blind, and cannot see afar off, and has forgotten that he was purged from his old sins. Therefore, brethren give rather diligence to make your calling and election sure: for if ye do these things, ye shall never fall. For by this means you shall enter abundantly into the everlasting kingdom of our Lord Jesus Christ," (2 Peter 1:5-11). Here Peter plainly affirms that they who have a faith that produces spiritual fruit come to an assurance that they are called of God and chosen to life and glory. To these, he gives assurance that they will never fail. For if a true, lively faith may fail and be wholly lost, what assurance can any man have that he is called of God and chosen to life eternal? How can the holy apostle say that if you do these things you shall never fall? It is because Christ reigns in all those who have the lively faith, and if his kingdom can be broken down again where it once existed, how can it be said in every respect to be eternal?

Now let us join these two passages together: that a man who has steadfast faith by which he resists the devil, can be sure that he is called and chosen and that he shall never fall. He that is firm and steadfast in a fruitful faith can be certain that they shall stand to the end. Otherwise, how can they be said to resist the devil if they are steadfast in the faith? When Paul tells us that the shield of faith quenches all the fiery darts of the devil, it is to give courage and comfort that once those have gained that shield, they shall never be overcome. For if their faith can be overcome, then it does not quench all Satan's fiery darts. When a man is steadfast in the faith, Satan is resisted. True faith assures the victory, no matter what assaults of Satan come his way. But if the outcome of the battle is doubtful, and it is believed that a faith may be lost, it discourages a man and takes away the comfort and consolation of assurance. Further, such a false belief removes what God has granted to his children, namely, that in all the trials, afflictions, and temptations which they pass through, they may have strong consolation. For it is written, "Wherein God wills to abundantly demonstrate to the heirs of promise the surety of his counsel confirmed by an oath, that by two immutable things in which it is impossible for God to lie, we might have strong consolation," (Heb. 6:17-18). If God confirms his promise by an oath that all they who believe in his Son shall have eternal life, we should come to the assurance of our salvation, for without such an assurance there can be no strong consolation. If men are condemned for high treason, and then some hope of pardon follows, it gives some comfort that they may escape the torments of death and not be executed. If there is doubt, they have no strong consolation; but when they know assuredly, and have it confirmed that they are set free by pardon, then is their consolation strong indeed.

  We are all condemned to hell to endure eternal torments because of our sin of high treason against God. Yet God has made a covenant and promise that as many as believe in the Son of God shall have free pardon, and so not only escape from those endless miseries, but also be lifted up into eternal glory. So those who wisely and sensibly consider this woeful, miserable state which we are all by nature partakers of, are filled with great horror and fear. For it is no light matter to be cast with the devil and his angels into eternal fire. And is he not then mad who can be merry so long as he is subject to so horrible a damnation?

There is hope of pardon, inasmuch as God has not only given his son to be a redeemer but has also promised with an oath that everyone who believes shall be saved. If a man feels that he has faith, this comforts him. But until he believes and knows that his faith is a true and lively faith that gains victory over Satan, he cannot have strong consolation that this same faith will never fail.

Eternal woe with the devil in hell is a terrifying thing, and so it is impossible for a man to have strong consolation unless he is sure he will be delivered from it. Not only that, a faith that the blessed Lord God has ordained that his children shall have strong consolation during the battle against Satan is a faith that brings assurance, knowing that faith can never be overcome. Take away the one and you take away the other.

So those who believe that true faith can be wholly lost overthrow the stability of God's covenant. And those who say that many have great gladness and consolation which do not possess true faith, I answer that the blind world is drowning in a carnal consolation. They neither soundly believe nor sensibly consider what estate they are actually in. They are as drunken men who do not realize they are headed for horrible torments but are rather merry and laugh and make sport of sin and carnal pleasures. If they truly considered the direction they were headed, it would surely dampen their merriness. This is not the strong consolation which the Holy Spirit speaks of. Theirs is a drunken madness. Those who truly possess a lively faith feel the power of Christ in them mortifying and slaying sin and quickening them to righteousness and true holiness. They desire to walk in the light and to bring forth the fruits and virtues of the Spirit. These have strong consolation and assurance that they will be delivered from hell, and made heirs of eternal glory, because they know that God sanctifies those he glorifies. And yet, such false teachers seek to misuse the holy scriptures to prove that the very reprobate can possess a true, lively, and justifying faith, which they also can utterly lose. In such circles, they also state that the very elect who possess the same true and lively faith for a time can also fall. If this is so, then all assurance is gone, and with all consolation.

Let us consider what their proof is, or what testimonies they stand upon to prove that true faith may be utterly lost. In the Old Testament it is written: "But when the righteous turn away from his righteousness and commit iniquity, and act according to all the abominations which the wicked do, should he live? All his righteous deeds which he has done shall not be remembered; for his transgression in which he transgresses, and for his sin in which he sins, for these he shall die," (Ezek. 18:24). The Lord Jesus says that there are some which believe for a time, and yet in time of temptation go away (Luke 8:1). You who stand by faith, Paul says, are not to be high minded, but fear (Rom. 11:20). The same apostle speaks of some that made shipwreck of the faith (1 Tim. 1:19). And "He that thinks he stands, let him take heed lest he fall," (1 Cor. 10:12). Christ said to the angel of the church of Ephesus, "Thou hast left thy first love," (Rev. 2:4). "Take heed lest any man fall away from the grace of God," (Heb. 12:15). And Peter states that such are like the dog that returns to his vomit (2 Peter 2:22). They use other scriptures to allegedly prove that men can have the true and lively faith and then wholly lose it. I will not answer everyone in particular, but in general.

Whenever the word of God speaks of falling from grace, or turning from the way of righteousness, or losing the faith, it is not speaking of the grace of sanctification or of the true, lively, justifying faith, but of another faith which the wicked may have and of those graces which they also after a sort are made partakers of. It is enough for me to show that whoever partakes of the lively faith can never lose that faith; he can never perish. For all the scriptures which they use to prove that faith can be lost is not speaking of that lively faith, or of those that are sanctified. For Christ said, "I am the true vine, and my father is the husbandman. Every branch in me that bears not fruit he takes away, and every branch in me that bears fruit he purges that it may bear more fruit," (John 15:1-2). Christ is the vine, and those who profess his name are the branches. These branches are of two sorts: the one bears no fruit, the other sort bears fruit. Now let it be known that the one which bears fruit is the one with the true and lively faith. These have been grafted into Christ and receive as it were the sap of life from him. Their faith is that of which Paul said "works by charity," and therefore everyone that has that faith bears fruit. What, then are those branches that do not bear fruit? They are those who are Christians in name and in profession only; otherwise he would not say, "Every branch in me that does not bear fruit…" They have also been grafted into Christ in as much as they have been baptized and do profess to believe in him. But their faith is a dead faith; otherwise *it could not be said* that they bear no fruit.

By this we see it is evident that there is a difference of faith, there is a fruitless or dead faith, and there is a faith which is lively and bears fruit. Every branch that bears fruit, that is, every one that has the true and lively faith, shall be purged, that it may bear more fruit. Therefore, none of the reprobate have the lively faith. This consequence is clear, if we consider that he says, "Every branch that bears fruit he purges, so that it may bear more fruit." Will they be so bold as to say that some branches that bear fruit shall be taken out of the vine, as well as the branches that bear no fruit? Or, will some branches that bear fruit be purged that they may bear more fruit, but in the end, they shall also be taken out of the vine? What difference is Christ making of the branches in regard to perseverance in the vine if any of the fruitful branches could be separated from it, as well as the unfruitful? This would not make sense for Christ to speak about it this way. They may even say that the holy scripture sometimes speaks in exceptions and in particulars, and so his saying is true although some branches that have born fruit can be taken out of the vine and afterward perish.

I answer that this is not the case here because our Savior is speaking universally as well as singularly. He said that not all the branches that are in me bear fruit, but every branch in me that bears fruit, he purges that it may bear more fruit. So, we may conclude that none of the reprobate actually possess the true and lively faith, for if they did, they would bring forth fruit and so remain forever in the vine. Again, whoever knows that he brings forth fruit, he may be assured that he shall continue in the vine forever; he shall never perish. Also, Christ said, "I am the bread of life, he that comes to me shall not hunger, and he that believes in me shall never thirst. This is the will of him that sent me, that everyone that sees the Son and believes in him may have everlasting life, and I will raise him up at the last day. I am that bread of life, which your fathers ate in the wilderness and are dead. This is that bread that came down from heaven, that if any man eat thereof, he should not die. I am the living bread which came down from heaven, if any man eat of this bread he shall live forever. He that eats my flesh and drinks my blood has eternal life: This is that bread which came down from heaven, not as your fathers did eat Manna, and are dead. He that eats of this bread shall live forever," (John 6:35-58). From these Scriptures we may draw a most firm conclusion, that not any one of the reprobates ever have had or can have the true and lively faith; but that whoever *believes,* he is assured of life eternal. Christ teaches that he is the bread of life, and that whoever eats of that bread shall live forever. It is not possible that any man should eat of that bread, and yet not live forever. Every one that believes in him (I speak of that lively faith by which we receive him and his benefits) partakes of his flesh and his blood. "He that believes in me shall *never* thirst."

Let a man show a reason why some that believe in Christ eat his flesh and drink his blood and others, having the same lively faith, do not. Will they say that the reprobate and damned who come to have the true and lively faith (according as they imagine) do indeed eat the flesh of Christ and drink his blood, and so for a time they are made lively members of Christ, even flesh of his flesh, and bones of his bones, as the apostle speaks in Ephesians 5:31? If they do not eat his flesh and drink his blood, then they do not have true faith. Remove that effect, and the cause is removed. If they affirm indeed that the reprobate do eat the flesh of Christ, so many of them as have the lively faith, then let them see how they overthrow the whole force of the argument of Christ, by which he proves that the Manna was not the bread of life; but that he himself is the bread of life. "Your fathers did eat manna in the wilderness and are dead. If any man eats of this bread, he shall live forever." How can this argument stand? Your fathers ate manna in the wilderness, and yet are dead in their sins. They are dead in spiritual and eternal death. Therefore, manna was not the bread of life that comes down from heaven. For of that some did eat, and yet died eternally. This proves this manna was in no way the bread of life. And how does Christ prove that he himself is the bread of life? "I am the bread which came down from heaven: if any man eats of this bread he shall live forever." In this way he reasons that whoever eats the flesh of Christ shall live forever. Therefore, the flesh of Christ is the bread of life. If they shall now say that some of the fathers in the wilderness ate the manna, and yet died in their sins, this cannot be denied. But Christ affirms that this manna was not the bread of life that comes down from heaven: and then adds their own saying, which is that some do eat the flesh of Christ, and yet die in their sins. But what is the logical conclusion if one thinks this way? Those who ate manna in the wilderness are dead. Therefore, manna was not the bread of life. If that is true, then this also should follow, that many that ate the flesh of Christ are yet damned; therefore, the flesh of Christ is not the bread of life. So those that affirm that any of the reprobate have the lively faith refute Christ.

To proceed, what can be firmer to prove that the reprobate cannot have the true, lively and justifying faith that Paul writes about? Foundationally, whoever has the true justifying faith has the Spirit of sanctification, the Spirit of adoption. As the apostle states, after you believed, you were "sealed with the holy Spirit of promise, the earnest of our inheritance, unto the redemption of the purchased possession, unto the praise of his glory," (Eph. 1:13-14).

Is there any so absurd as to believe that a man is a lively member of Jesus Christ, possessing justifying faith, and yet does not have the Holy Spirit of promise, that Spirit of adoption, that seal, and that pledge? If they say that the faith which the reprobate attains is without this Spirit of adoption, or without this seal or pledge, then the faith of the reprobate is not the true justifying and sanctifying faith which purges the heart (Acts 15). Regarding the Spirit of adoption, see what the apostle says, "As many as are led by the Spirit of God, they are the sons of God. For ye have not received the spirit of bondage again to fear; but ye have received the Spirit of adoption, whereby we cry 'Abba, Father.' That same Spirit bears witness with our spirit that we are the sons of God," (Rom. 8.14-16). If any of the reprobate are led by the Spirit of God, or are at any time sanctified, then as Paul says here truly, that "as many as are led by the Spirit of God, *they are the sons of God.*" Some of the reprobate taste the heavenly power, but they are not led with the Spirit of God, they are not sanctified, they do not walk after the Spirit. Moreover, the Spirit of adoption, the sanctifying Spirit which is in all that have the true, lively and justifying faith, bears witness with the spirit of believers, that they are the children of God. This is the lively faith when a man believes that the Lord God is his Father and that he is the son of God. And this faith is not separate from the Spirit of adoption, for it is on his testimony that they do believe, and by him they cry "Abba, Father."

Is not this Spirit a true spirit? And is not his witness most firm and true? Why might a person say that a man that has true faith, that is to say, he believes by the testimony of the Holy Spirit that God is his Father, and yet he is indeed the child of the devil? And moreover, does not the apostle say that after they believed they were sealed with the Holy Spirit of promise? This seal is much more than even the mere testimony of the Spirit. Can this seal be disannulled or broken or made void? Is this seal untrue? If their opinion is true, no man can say, "God has sealed me with his Spirit, therefore I belong to God." For if a reprobate also has that seal, and it fails him, then who can say that the seal is true and infallible?

John showed us on what testimonies faith in Christ is grounded when he said, "There are three that bear record in heaven: the Father, the Word, and the Holy Spirit, and these three are one. And there are three that bear record in earth: the spirit, and water, and blood, and these three agree in one. If we receive the testimony of men, the testimony of God is greater: For this is the witness which he testified of his son. He that believeth in the son of God has the witness in himself,"

(1 John 5:7-10). What is the purpose of all these witnesses but to give *assurance* of faith? And if these witnesses testify to a man that he is the child of God and shall be saved (for every one that has the true and lively faith has it upon the testimony of all these witnesses) and yet he is a reprobate, then is not the witness of God greater than the witness of men? Also, to what end should he mention all these witnesses? It is because they give an absolute testimony that everyone who believes has everlasting life.

  The holy Scriptures show how the reprobate cannot partake of the sanctifying faith because they are not led at any time by the Spirit of adoption, they are not sealed with the Holy Spirit of promise, and they do not have the witness of God within them. Whoever has these things, let him be assured that he is sanctified, he is justified, he will be glorified, and he shall never perish (Rom. 8:32). And this is what the holy Scripture in many places proclaims, that whoever believes in the son of God, he shall never be confounded.

  But what if the reprobate never had true faith nor the Spirit of adoption? Even the elect sins and falls, which seems to indicate that there is no spark of true faith in them at the time. This is a trick of the devil to uproot the stability and foundation of the truth. But the word of God teaches that whoever is regenerate and born of God by the new and spiritual birth, which is everyone that possesses true faith, *he is a new creature.* Such a man cannot fall so far that this new birth could be extinguished in him. For this we have the testimony uttered by John in these words, "Whoever is born of God does not sin, for his seed remains in him, neither can he sin, because he is born of God," (1 John 3:9) Also, "we know that whoever is born of God does not sin, that one is begotten of God, and that wicked one cannot touch him," (1 John 5:18). In the former verses, there are two members and a reason for each of them to confirm the same: that whoever is born of God does not sin, for his seed remains in him (the first reason). And then the second, "Neither can he sin, because he is born of God," (which is the second reason).

So those who hold that a regenerate man may lose the faith and be utterly void of the Spirit of sanctification refutes the scripture. For first, John says that whoever is born of God does not sin. They say that a man who sins has his faith utterly quenched and is wholly deprived of the spirit of adoption. But he that is born of God cannot continue in sin if he continues born of God. If an unregenerate man is born of God through a true and lively faith, and yet falls into sin, then he sins while he is in that state. For he first casts away his faith and the grace of the sanctifying Spirit, and then he commits sin. But see how John meets all arguments with his reasoning that those who are born of God do not sin because God's seen remains in him.

What is this seed of God which remains in all that are born of God? The word of God is called the *incorruptible seed* by which God *begets* his children (1

Peter 1:23). That word is but an instrument; the Holy Spirit is the *worker* of the new birth. And therefore, our Savior teaches that except a man is born again of water and of the Spirit he cannot enter into the kingdom of God (John 3:5). The seed of God then is the graces of the sanctifying Spirit and the lively word. Those men that say a man may lose his faith and the Spirit of sanctification speak contrary to what the holy apostle here spoke. The seed of God remains in all those who are born of God, John states, and therefore they do not sin. They do not sin that deadly sin of falling from God or of being separated from Christ.

Of course, if their saying is true, there is no seed of God which remains in those who do wholly lose their faith and in whom the sanctifying graces are utterly extinguished. It may be that they will here again say that the seed of God remains in them so long as they are born of God, and hold the faith, and stand in grace. And yet John speaks absolutely, that whoever is born of God, the seed of God ever after remains in him: and therefore, he does not sin. For when he says his seed remains in them, we must know that it remains in them forever. If the seed of God remains forever in the regenerate, then the sanctifying Spirit remains in them forever also. For these cannot be separated.

But to remove all doubt, and to minister sound comfort and strong consolation to all that have the true and lively faith, even to let them that know indeed and understand for certainty that they cannot perish, that they cannot be overcome by Satan in the battle, he adds, "Neither can he sin." In this way, he confirms it with this reason: *because he is born of God.* What can they say to this? How will they avoid this? Will they say that John meant here some other matter? Is it not clearer than the sun, that the regenerate cannot wholly be deprived of faith nor of the Spirit of sanctification when he says they cannot sin? Oh how happy and blessed is the state and condition of that man which has attained to the true and lively faith, in whom is the Spirit of sanctification by which he is led, even the Spirit of adoption that bears witness with his spirit that he is the child of God, seeing he may be tempted and at various times be led into sin. Still it is impossible that he should fall from God.

And what is the reason by which he proves that he cannot fall? *Because he is born of God.* Consider where the force of this reason lies. Men are mortal, their seed is corruptible, and that which is born of man is corruptible and mortal. God is incorruptible and immortal, and so the seed of God is called incorruptible seed and immortal. Therefore, it follows that the birth which is of God is incorruptible and immortal. Where the life of God is, it cannot be extinguished. Do not think it strange then when John says the regenerate cannot sin. Except they will deny the manifest and clear testimonies of the word of God: except they will affirm that the seed of God is corruptible and so decays, and does not abide in those that are begotten of God. Except they will also make the testimony of the Spirit of adoption false, and finally, except they will make the seal of God and the pledge which he gives of no effect, we can know that our calling and election is sure, and from such we can draw strong consolation.

Let them renounce this error, that the true and lively faith and the sanctifying Spirit may be in the reprobate, and that the same lively faith and quickening grace may be wholly put out for a time in the elect. It may be demanded that seeing the word of God is so evident that men are to resist the devil steadfast in the faith, being fully assured that he who once attained the lively faith can never be overcome nor perish, why do some hold that true faith and the spirit of adoption may be had and lost again? *What would drive them to such absurdities?*

They would have it be in man's own will and power that he receives faith and the whole work of regeneration. They would have it be in the power and will of man to retain the same faith and sanctifying spirit. Why are they of that mind? Is it because they are *jealous* that God should have the whole praise and glory for man's salvation, as man being unable to do anything to obtain the grace that is wholly of God? We cannot say. But it is another thing that drives them to this, and that is this: they take it that unless it is in man's will and power to receive and to retain faith, it will follow from a higher cause, such as God has chosen them to life, to those he gives faith and works in them by his Spirit the new birth. Man in his own power cannot attain to true faith and regeneration, and is therefore ordained to eternal destruction. It seems to follow, then, that there is a predestination, an eternal decree of God, by which he chooses and ordains some to life everlasting and appoints others to eternal destruction.

This doctrine, they say, charges God with injustice and cruelties. For what is crueler than purposefully creating and then choosing that some of his creatures are condemned to eternal torments? Where is, they ask, the infinite mercy, the justice and goodness of God? To charge the Lord God with any cruelty or injustice is most wicked, blasphemous, and abominable. And therefore they hold this the safest course for the defense of the justice and mercy of God, where the word of God speaks of election, that *God* has chosen to life eternal all those whom he did foresee would receive the faith, walk in obedience and continue to the end, and so their faith, good works and perseverance which God foresaw is the cause that moved the Lord to choose them. On the other side, he has also foreseen that they either would not receive the faith at all, or else after they have received it, of their own wickedness they would fall from it utterly and finally, and so in his foreknowledge he ordained them to damnation. This, they say, stands to reason.

What shall we say to this? Shall we here enter to discourse on the scriptures regarding election and reprobation? I have no such purpose. But only so far as agrees with our present matter, namely, to make it appear that the steadfastness of our faith, and the full assurance of our salvation, depends on the knowledge of our election. Namely, if we find in us the true and lively faith, which goes with the Spirit of sanctification, we may then rise up to that high cause and be assured that the Lord has in his eternal and unchangeable decree chosen us in Christ to be his children, so that we cannot perish.

    To come then to an answer to those men: is not this a strange thing, that they will comprehend by reason how God could decree the choice or election of some of his creatures to life, and the reprobation of others to eternal destruction for their sins unjustly? The apostle asks, "But who art thou oh man that pleads with God?" They answer that they do not plead with God, but they stand for the defense of the justice and mercy of God, lest it should be imputed to him that which is unjust and cruel. Is not this to plead with God, or against God? When he shall be just, he shall be good, he shall be merciful, no further reason can we comprehend. He must yield a reason sufficient for your understanding and capacity, with what right or equity he could do so, or else you will reject it. Is not this, I say, to plead against God?

    Paul, after he disputed the rejecting of Christ by the Jews and the calling in of the Gentiles, breaks forth into this exclamation, "Oh the depth of the riches both of the wisdom and knowledge of God: how unsearchable are his judgments and his ways past finding out!" (Rom.

11:33). To this the prophet in the Psalm agrees, saying "Thy judgments are as the great deep," (Psalm 36:6). Let it be demanded, what judgments of God are unsearchable, or as the great deep? Are they not those judgments which he executes on his creatures, and especially on his chief creatures, angels, and men? If his judgments are as the great deep, unsearchable and incomprehensible both to men and angels, then it is in the highest matter that he has ordained by his eternal decree to bestow eternal life and glory on some, and to appoint others to eternal torments, which they shall endure justly for their sins. For if any judgments of God are unsearchable, it is in predestination. It may be rightly said, that if the counsels, ways, and judgements of God are not unsearchable in that eternal decree, then there is no judgment of God that is unsearchable. And this would be to deny not only the saying of the apostle and of the prophet, but also after a sort to deny God, for he that will make his judgments searchable, makes God himself to be searchable.

Will you measure and comprehend the counsels, the decrees, and the judgments of God by reason? Then measure and comprehend God himself, even that eternal and infinite majesty, with the same reason. Now if it is so, that God chose some for this cause because he did foresee that of their own will and power they would be faithful, do good works and continue to the end as well as those who would be unfaithful, wicked, and rebellious even to their death, and those in his foreknowledge he saw to be justly damned, there is nothing incomprehensible in these judgments. For your reason finds out, and your understanding comprehends all causes, and you can show a reason how God has done everything, and yet is just. Yes, all the causes of his counsels he opens to you, if this is so.

Why then did Paul cry out, "How unsearchable are his judgments!" Why did the prophet also say that his judgments are deep? It seems the prophet was dull of understanding, as was Paul, for you have entered into this great deep, and with the light of reason searched out all things. And whatever is not agreeable to your reason, you cast out of God's decrees. For nothing must stand higher than your reason can reach and comprehend. You say that whatever is contrary to reason is absurd. But take heed that you do not extol reason too much, though it adheres to the principles of logic. But to think that it can rise up to comprehend God and his eternal decree is extreme folly. If we look at particulars, we shall find it to be so. We believe and confess that the Lord God by his eternal power and infinite wisdom created heaven and earth, and all things which are in them, both visible and invisible. Of the invisible creatures in heaven, some of the angels sinned and fell. These God condemned to eternal fire, and they are now devils. Others (whom the holy apostle calleth the elect angels) never sinned, neither shall any of them ever sin, but shall remain very glorious and blessed forever.

Tell me now, were not all these the creatures of God, created in the same estate and condition? Why, then, did some of them stand, and others fall? Will you not say that of his infinite goodness and love, he decreed to hold up the one, so that they should never sin nor be in danger of falling, while decreeing to leave those others to their own will and power? Why did he not show the same goodness and love towards all? Why did he set such glorious creatures in such a place from which they could fall from heavenly glory into devil's torments? Was he not able to support them, to retain them in glory with the rest? He created man in great dignity, even after his own image. Why did he not keep him in that estate? Why did he allow the devil to enter into the woman and to tempt her? Why did he not forewarn the man and the woman, that such an enemy would attack them? Or why did he not give them the strength to gain the victory in that temptation? Will you say that God only allowed those things to be done by the devil, and that he did not ordain that any of these should happen, for that cannot stand with equity or justice and does not agree with mercy. If you have a child, when it is in your power to allow, will you willingly let a lion come and devour him? And who would agree that it was enough to clear you from cruelty to say that you did not decree it, you only allowed it to happen? If this excuse is no defense, how foolish are you to use it in defense of the justice and mercy of God? Will you call the justice of God and his mercy under the account of your reason, that you may by your own wit comprehend it, or else it cannot be justice?

How much better is it that you should cry out with the apostle, "How unsearchable are his judgments!" And where you cannot comprehend by reason how God should in justice either decree or allow the fall of angels and men, to rest in this, that though we cannot comprehend those things, yet we are sure there can be no unrighteousness with God. Whatever he decrees is most holy and just, for his will is the perfect rule of all righteousness.

To proceed, when man fell, and cast himself and all his posterity into endless misery, a Redeemer was promised. All are alike lost; there are none that are in themselves better or more worthy than another. So why, then, is not the Redeemer sent to all? If any shall reply to say he was sent to all, that is untrue. For God chose the seed of Abraham, the nation of the Jews. He separated them from all other nations of the world. He gave them his laws and ordinances, even the lively *oracles* to teach them. At the same time, he left the other nations in the dark, to walk in the vanities of their own mind, subject to the manifold illusions and slights of devils, for many ages, among whom there were many famous wise men, philosophers, poets and orators. Yes, there were among them a great number which could never hear of Christ, perishing in their native corruption, that is, in original sin. Who can search out and comprehend the judgments of God in this? Were they not the work of his hands as well? Yet there is no hope offered them.

But in the fullness of time, Christ Jesus, the only light and salvation of the world, is preached to the Gentiles. Why did he not then open the eyes of all? Why did he not give that effectual grace of his Spirit to all who believe in his Son to salvation? When he opened the heart of Lydia, why did he not also open the hearts of the rest that heard Paul preach? Some will say it is because they would not. And yet, of those who were most unwilling, God made willing where it pleased him. We have a perfect example in Paul, who was a cruel persecutor of Christians. Christ said, "No man comes unto me except the father which sent me draw him," (John 6). Why did he not draw Herod, and Pilate, and the high priests, as well as Paul? We see in these latter days that there are great nations, like the West Indies, which had never heard of Christ until lately, and then they were invaded by cruel and idolatrous people who murdered them, so that they were made to stumble and to move even further from Christ. Who can comprehend the depth of these judgments?

Shall we not lay down the pride of our own understanding and say with the apostle, "Hath not the potter power over the clay, of the same lump to make one vessel unto honor and another unto dishonor? Or shall the thing formed say to him that formed it, 'Why hast thou made me thus?'" O beloved, let us lay aside all such vain and curious presumptions, and let us, as the holy Scripture directs us, make our singular comfort that eternal decree of God with which we are to fortify ourselves against the devil. God of his own good will has chosen in his son Jesus Christ, before the foundations of the world were laid, those whom he will save as the heirs of eternal glory. He has in his predetermined time redeemed them, not with gold or precious stones (as Peter said) but with the blood of his son, as of a Lamb immaculate and without spot. Those whom he called, he also sanctified. This decree of God is unchangeable, as it is impossible that any of his elect should perish. Who can pluck them out of the hands of Christ?

For these reasons, we can be assured that none can have true faith but the chosen of God for none receives the spirit of adoption which witnesses with their spirit that they are the children of God but the elect. The elect are those regenerate who are born of God and sealed with the Holy Spirit of promise.

Let us now come down to your own self. Can you truly say, "I have the lively faith, I have received the Spirit of adoption, which witnesses with my spirit that I am the child of God; I am regenerate, I have the true repentance, I am sanctified. Satan tempts me strongly in many ways, but I am sure that he shall never get the victory over me."

Is this not a singular comfort to a man? If any that have the Spirit of adoption may lose him, then where is the steadfastness of faith which Peter here requires in resisting the devil? If we depend on ourselves, we cannot be undoubtedly sure and steadfast; we may well waver and doubt. But when we know that we are kept by the power of God, as is written in 1 Peter 1, then we have a rock on which to rest, a rock on which we can stand steadfast and armed with the power of God.

This faith may be tried, and may seem oftentimes to be shaken, but it can never be overcome. Some will say that every man cannot come to know that he has received the true and lively faith, or the Spirit of adoption, for we have seen many say they believe the gospel, thinking that they have the true faith and sanctifying Spirit, and yet in time they fall away.

It is true that there are many which embrace the gospel and profess it with such feeling that they suppose God has called them as his children. There is for a time such a moving in their hearts, and yet in time they manifest themselves not to be of God. One occasion or another drives them away, so that some of them become heretics, and some of them fall into vices, and become so pagan that all the former graces which they had tasted of vanish and are lost.

Therefore, Peter urges us to make our calling and election sure. For seeing the reprobate receives a kind of faith and zeal which yet is not the true and lively faith, we are willed to be diligent and careful to see that we do not rest in that faith. We must labor to attain that testimony of the Spirit of adoption. We must seek to be confirmed and even sealed with the Holy Spirit of promise, and so come to that full assurance of faith and hope which never fails.

This is what Peter is teaching when he tells us to add virtue to our faith, and knowledge to our virtue, *etc.* For if we follow that rule which he prescribes, we shall be sure never to fall. We shall with a steadfast faith resist our adversary the devil and get the victory over him. As this is such a matter of great importance, I pray and implore you, as you care for the state of your own souls, that you set your hearts on the lively oracles of God, seeking day and night after the knowledge of holy things and how to please the Lord your God. Then shall you be blessed for evermore, Amen.

FINIS

Other Helpful Works Published by Puritan Publications

Taking Hold of Eternal Life in Christ
by George Gifford (1547-1620)

Is holiness of life a necessary prerequisite for getting into heaven? Do you have the power as a Christian to overcome sin? What has Jesus Christ done in enabling you to live righteously according to his commandments? How do you successfully glorify Jesus Christ in your daily walk?

The Christian's Combat Against the Devil
by Christopher Love (1618-1651)

Are you ready for battle? In the evil day will you stand firm? Do you have on the whole armor of God? What is your strategy for spiritual warfare? Listen to Mr. Love's excellent treatise in MP3 format or read it in book form.

The Glorious Name of God the Lord of Hosts
by Jeremiah Burroughs (1599-1646)

One of the most glorious and often used names throughout the Bible is THE LORD OF HOSTS. What does that name mean, and why is it so often used? Burroughs shows that it is most glorious!

The Nature, Danger and Cure of Temptation
by Richard Capel (1586–1656)

In this masterful treatise on temptation, Capel explains that God's honor is on the line, and what will Christians do to uphold his honor amidst those temptations? Will they give in easily, or do they know how to fight?

The Armor of God
by Paul Bayne (1573-1617)

You are in a spiritual war if you are a professing Christian. Are you prepared for it? Paul Bayne teaches you how to wear God's armor for victory in Christ.

The Growth and Spreading of Heresy
by Thomas Hodges (1600-1672)

How does heresy invade Christ's church, and grow? Thomas Hodges shows how heresy grows and spreads, and what Christians can do to guard against it in this rare puritan work.

The Natural Man Directed to Jesus Christ
by Francis Roberts (1609-1675)

Robert's work is one of the greatest pieces of puritan sermonizing on original sin, depravity and conversion. If you are aware of Alleine's "An Alarm to the Unconverted," you will find Robert's masterpiece even more convincing and powerful. This is the book to not only read and reread yourself, but also to hand out to family members and friends who still remain in their natural state. It is exquisite puritan evangelism at its best.

The Christian's Duty to Walk Wisely
by Matthew Mead (1630-1699)

This is, no doubt, one of the best works we've ever published. In a simple and easy to follow manner, in two parts, Mead teaches Christians how to fight against Satan's temptations, and walk wisely in the trials that come to them from God. Secondly, he also shows the Christian how to love Christ more, and love the world less. This is a rare puritan work, and ought to be required reading for every Christian who desires to combat the world, the flesh and devil so that they might walk wisely before God.

A Discourse on the Damned Art of Witchcraft
by William Perkins (1558-1602)

Are you in league with Satan? Are you unknowingly in covenant with the devil? How affected is your house with superstition and witchcraft? You would be surprised! William Perkins delivers a valuable treatise on the subject.

www.ingramcontent.com/pod-product-compliance
Lightning Source LLC
Chambersburg PA
CBHW070207100426
42743CB00013B/3086